# BAIRDY'S GONNA
# GET YA!
## The Ian Baird Story

# BAIRDY'S GONNA
# GET YA!
## The Ian Baird Story

## Marc Bracha

DB PUBLISHING

Cover image courtesy of Andrew Varley.

This edition published in Great Britain in 2013 by DB Publishing, an imprint of JMD Media.

Copyright © Marc Bracha 2013

ISBN 9781780913025

Printed and bound by Copytech (UK) Limited, Peterborough.

# Contents

This book is dedicated to Ian's parents Pat & Hilary, his son Liam, daughter Amy and my father Phillip who introduced me, as a young boy, to a wonderful place in LS11 called Elland Road.

# Foreword

During my first spell as manager of Leeds United, my chief scout Tony Faw-throp recommended to me a young centre-forward who was playing with Southampton. His name was Ian Baird. Although born in Yorkshire, Ian started his career with the south coast club. We managed to sign him for £50,000 and that was the start of Ian's association with Leeds United Football Club.

His aggression, work rate, whole-hearted attitude and skill made him very popular with the fans. In his first period with the club he worked under me, and then under the ex-Leeds United captain and legend Billy Bremner.

In his early days at Leeds, Ian had to work hard to curb his naturally aggressive attitude to the game, and he found himself getting into hot water with the officials on numerous occasions. But that was all part of Ian's makeup as a player – big, strong and fearless in the air, with a good touch on the ball. He was, to me, a throwback to an old-fashioned type of centre-forward. In a way, he reminded me of a young Joe Jordan, and when you are talking about centre-forwards, I don't think I could pay Ian a bigger compliment.

Although I never worked with Ian for a long period of time, as I was relieved of my duties at the club, it was a pleasure to have him at Elland Road. I loved the way he worked hard at all aspects of his game, and that is one of the reasons he had a long and distinguished career in football. Ian was one of a number of young players at the club who played without fear, and his love of football was evident right from the start.

He achieved cult status at Leeds United, ironically leaving the first time to join Portsmouth, arch rivals of his first club Southampton. The fee was £285,000, a fair profit on what we paid for him, and I know Ian relished that challenge. Struggling financially, Portsmouth sold him back to Leeds United in a cut-price deal.

Ian was successful once again, picking up the Leeds United Supporters Club Player of the Year award in 1989. Following the arrival of Lee Chapman he moved on to Middlesbrough, for £500,000, although his involvement with Leeds United didn't end there. If anything, he became an even bigger hero at Leeds, scoring two goals for Middlesbrough against Newcastle United on the last day of the season – which with a win at Bournemouth clinched Leeds' promotion. Ian picked up a Second Division championship winner's medal, due to the number of games he had played for Leeds earlier that season.

Ian played for numerous clubs throughout his career, but I think he would say, that his most enjoyable and successful times were spent in West Yorkshire, and I know that in the history of the club Ian will always remain an iconic figure for the passion and commitment he gave to the cause.

I will always look back with fond memories to the short time I worked with Ian. He was fun to be around, his enthusiasm on the training pitch and his approach to games was second to none and when he comes back to visit Elland Road, he always gets the type of welcome he deserves, as a much loved ex-Leeds United player.

Eddie Gray MBE
June, 2013

# Acknowledgements

Firstly, I wish to thank the man himself. Without his approval, assistance and support this project would not have been possible. It is a great honour to say that I am Ian Baird's official biographer. Thank you, Ian.

Secondly, I wish to give a special thank you to Leeds United legend, Eddie Gray MBE for agreeing to write the foreword for the book. The word legend is used all too freely these days but when you use the phrase in its intended form, you will not find many bigger Leeds United legends than Eddie.

I would also like to thank the publisher, Steve Caron, the Editor, Rick Briggs and the Designer, Simon Hartshorne. These guys have shown faith in me and made all the hard work worthwhile. In addition, a special mention for Mick Leonard who provided me with some vital insight with regards to Ian's time over in Hong Kong.

Thank you to the various newspapers and journalists who have provided me with information on Ian's career. Leon Wobschall, Paul Robinson and the Yorkshire Evening Post, John Helm, Doug O'Kane and the Barnsley Chronicle, Don Veale, John Wray, Jez Gale at the Daily Echo, Anthony Brown, Anthony Vickers and the Middlesbrough Gazette, Neil Cameron at the Sunday Sun and Dave Woods, the Bristol City historian

Also a thank you to Katherine Hannah, Adam Pope and everybody at BBC Radio Leeds for letting us promote the book on West Yorkshire Sport, live from Elland Road on the night that Leeds United played Chesterfield in August 2013.

In addition, I will never forget the help, support and encouragement I received from Jon Howe, Eddie Taylor, Gary Edwards, David Saffer, David Watkins and Paul Dews which proved to be invaluable.

Throughout the project I have spoken to many people, who have been involved in Ian's life, and supporters of various clubs who have provided me with their memories. I thank each and every one of them, in no particular order for their contributions. If I have missed anybody, please accept my apologies:

John Sheridan, Micky Adams, Bernie Slaven, Patrick Bushell, Richard Hargrave, Michael Durkin, Matt Thompson, Glen Downing, Bobby Davison, Paul Downer, Brendan Ormsby, John McClelland, John Stiles, Lorna Tinker, Daz King from the Vital Leeds website, Graham Bell, Will Jago, Mike McGeary, Dave Simpson, Mark Absolon, Paul Sweet, Jim Platt of the Middlesbrough ex players Association, Paul Dunham, Mandy Ronchetti, Dave Todd, Steve Duly, James Hobbs, Mark Storey, John 'Happy' Hendrie, Paul Camillin, Tim Carder, Gordon White, Duncan Holley, Mel Sterland, Craig Maskell, Mel Booth, Hilary Attard, Alan Kernaghan, Alan Knight, Johnny Westwood, Steve Gritt, Stuart Storer, Keith Hill, Simon Coleman, Glyn Snodin, Neil Harle, David Harle, Tom Jordan, Tim Manns, Antony Ramm, Joe Jordan, John Robertson, Craig Levein, Gary Bennett, Mike Whitlow, David Armstrong, John Pearson – 'The Big-Bird', Mike Milligan, Lawrie McMenemy, Wayne Allison, Mark Gavin, Peter Lorimer, Gary Mackay, Darren Baird, Dave Martin – 'The Diesel', Dylan Kerr, Gary Owers, Kerry Mayo, Jimmy Lumsden, Hayden Evans, Andy Ritchie, Peter Shilton, Nick Buxton, Mick Jones, Tony Fawthrop, Giles Watkins, Hilary Baird, Jeremy Hilton, Martin Gale, Paul Thorpe, Ian Curtis, Alan Curtis, Pat Heard, Gordon Strachan, Steve Rhodes, Andrew Varley, Dean Walls, Vince Hilaire, John Anderson, Shaun Wilkinson, Adi Aymes, Pat Baird, Gareth Howells, Matt Gray, Melvyn Flower, Christina Baird, David Howells, Phil Pairpoint, Chris Waddle, Lyndon Simmonds, Dave Cocker, Anthony Clavane, Richard Dryden, Martin Foyle, Mick Hewitt, Steve at Greens on Screen, Penny Rudkin at Southampton Library, George Parris, Simon Lynch, Gavin Baird, Tracy Roe, Lesley Lowman, Dennis Bundy, John Buckley, Andrew Dalton, Mickey Thomas, Lorna Hartwell at the England Schools Football Association, Ray Fell, Julian Barker, Scott Sellars, Ralph Ineson, Alex Kickham, Keith James & John Mann at the Welsh Schoolboy Football Association, Marcus Hackney, Tommy Wright, Pete Cooney, Amy Baird, Dave Malone, Liam Baird, Steve Brookwell, Gordon White, Pete Cormack, Becky Lickley, Kevin Blackwell, Tom Olding, Reuben Agboola, Jason Hill, Russell Vaughan, Chris Webb, Andy Wilson, Andy Johnson and David Smith.

# A labour of love

In 1985 when Ian Baird signed for Leeds United, football was not the fashionable spectacle that it is today. Sky TV's millions, which transformed our national sport, were still many years away.

As far as Leeds United were concerned, the club was not in the best condition – on or off the field. The terraces were crumbling, crowd trouble was commonplace and attendances had dropped alarmingly. But Ian Baird, along with John Sheridan, gave everybody hope in what was a testing period for a club that had fallen on hard times. The two of them were hero-worshipped. Every Leeds United supporter from that period wishes we had a Bairdy and a Shez in today's team.

I will always remember 11 Leeds players, managed by Neil Warnock, leaving the field after a dreadful 2-0 defeat at Yorkshire neighbours Barnsley during the miserable 2012-13 season. The majority of them never looked at or acknowledged the fans, camped in the away end at Oakwell. It was as if it they didn't care. But when the team that Bairdy played in suffered a defeat, it hurt. Those players cared and they shared our disappointments.

For those of us who watched Ian Baird in his pomp, we are left with many memories of crunching tackles, gritted teeth and clenched fists. His goal-scoring celebration was trademark and everybody inside Elland Road – particularly the fans on the Kop, on the Lowfields or in the South Stand – idolised the aggressive nature and determined style of the centre-forward, plucked from the fringes of Southampton's first team in 1985. He was looked on as one of our own. His desire and contribution to the cause will always be appreciated and never forgotten by those of us who were around to follow Leeds United in that decade.

Also, he protected his own and whenever a Leeds player was clattered by an opponent, a rousing chant would lift from the Kop, warning the offender what was coming... 'Bairdy's gonna get ya!'

However, in the midst of bookings, sendings off and trips to face the wrath of the authorities for disciplinary problems, Ian Baird had a real talent to play football. For a big man he had a great touch. He could pick a pass out, he would win his aerial duels, he had the ability to hold the ball up and bring others into play. His work rate could never be questioned – and more importantly, he scored goals. Former colleagues of Ian's were quick to stress how important he was to the team, and what a good player he could be when he kept a lid on his temper and curbed his aggression.

When Ian left Leeds United for the second time in February 1990, I was gutted. Although he found goals hard to come by during the first half of the promotion season, he remained in the side. That side was top of the league, that side was winning games, and Bairdy had created many goals for his team-mates with Bobby Davison being the main benefactor.

On the day that Bairdy made his debut for Middlesbrough, Leeds didn't have a game as they were scheduled to play the following day at Swindon Town. I travelled from Doncaster to Ayresome Park and stood on the Holgate End. His new club was playing Portsmouth and I didn't care who won the game. I just wanted to see Bairdy score.

The highest accolade that Ian Baird could receive from his time at Middlesbrough came from one of their most popular players ever, who scored goals for fun. Bernie Slaven, the Republic of Ireland international striker, told me that he regards Ian as the best centre-forward he ever played alongside at club level. I told Bairdy of the praise bestowed on him by Slaven and he just nodded and replied, "I should think so, I did all his running for a season and a half." Deep down, I sensed Ian was bursting with pride.

It was on the 21st of April 2012 that I contacted Ian Baird via an email to Eastleigh Football Club. In that email was my offer to put Ian's career and life in writing but in all honesty, I did not expect a response.

Less than 24 hours later, Ian himself replied, sending me his mobile number with the request that I contact him. His initial thought was that somebody was taking the piss, but after a few conversations he had warmed to the idea and gave me the thumbs up. I was ecstatic and immediately started my research. Ian Baird had given me the opportunity of a lifetime.

Five months before I made contact with Bairdy, my partner Sharon gave birth to our twins, Frankie and Ellie. Sharon has been an absolute rock throughout, giving me encouragement as I worked around the clock putting this book together.

The honour of meeting Ian for the first time came on the 8th of June 2012; we met outside Liverpool St Station on a typical summer's day in London. The rain was bouncing as we quickly made our way to a little cafe/bar called the White Hart, where over a few coffees and beers; Ian commenced to tell me how it all began. It seemed unbelievable that I was sitting with a guy who had played so many games and scored many goals for Leeds United. A guy idolised by so many people across the world, to the extent that he was voted amongst the best 100 players that have played for the club.

I have lost count of the number of emails I have sent and read. I have lost count of the number of phone calls I have made and received. I have lost count of how many times I travelled to London to meet Ian but every single moment of writing this book has been magical.

Ian tells it how it was, a full blooded account of his life. In addition to his playing career, he talks openly about a turbulent ending to his time in Hong Kong and the frustrations of football management.

Whoever you support, whether Ian played for your team or not, I am sure you will find Ian's story fascinating. It is one riddled with humorous stories, good fortune, bad luck and heartbreak.

I hope you enjoy reading the book as much as I have writing it.

Marching on Together.
Marc Bracha

# Introduction

Saturday the 2nd of December, 1989. On a bitterly cold winter's afternoon in front of 31,715 expectant fans, Leeds United were entertaining promotion rivals Newcastle United at Elland Road. It was just before a packed Christmas schedule – and with Leeds, Sheffield United and Newcastle making the running at the top of the Second Division, points were proving increasingly valuable.

The game, a tense, typically robust encounter, remained goalless until the 70th minute.

The Leeds captain Gordon Strachan collected the ball and the passage of play, as described at the time by Yorkshire Television commentator John Helm, neatly encapsulates the appeal of Ian Baird.

*"Strachan for Leeds switches the point of play. Jones, over the top, this is dangerous. Sterland... there's the cross for Ian Baird... WHAT A GOAL FOR LEEDS!!! And if anybody deserves it today it's Ian Baird. He's given everything and he's got everything now."*

That goal, a superb header in front of a packed Gelderd End, gave Leeds a 1-0 win and it was sweet revenge for a 5-2 hammering at St James' Park in the blazing sunshine of the season's opening day. It also earned the Yorkshire club a vital three points in a season that would see them finish as Champions of the old Second Division, sealing a long overdue return to the top flight from which they had been relegated in May 1982.

Mel Sterland, who put the ball over which Baird headed home, later announced that he had suffered a cracked rib in a clash with Kevin Brock. But in determined fashion, he powered his way down the right-hand side in front of the Lowfields to get his cross in. The reward was invaluable, and Baird milked the applause with his trademark goal celebration:

"It was a fantastic moment in front of the Kop. Although I had played well that season, the goals were hard to come by but I certainly enjoyed that one."

Strike partner Bobby Davison was also pleased to see the ball settling in the back of John Burridge's goal:

"I was chuffed for Bairdy, he worked extremely hard. He was a great strike partner who was under-rated. Everyone at Leeds appreciated the work he did and what he was about. It was a superb goal that won us a game we were desperate to win, especially after the opening-day defeat at St James' Park."

Leeds United fans everywhere idolised Ian Baird, and many have recalled that fantastic winning goal against Newcastle as his finest moment whilst plying his trade in West Yorkshire.

Nobody realised on the day, but it would be the last time that Ian Baird scored for Leeds United before a £500,000 move took him to Middlesbrough following Howard Wilkinson's signing of Lee Chapman.

Ian Baird's story has many ups and downs. It is a fascinating journey that started in the South Yorkshire town of Rotherham on Wednesday the 1st of April 1964 – when Ian, the first child of Pat and Hilary Baird, was born.

# 1

## An early obsession with football

Ian's parents married in 1963 after meeting at a dinner and dance held at Doncaster Racecourse after its showpiece event, The St Leger.

Before meeting Pat, Hilary had progressed through a theatrical boarding school to become a classical ballet dancer. She displayed her talents in shows all over the world, but when she was back in her hometown of Doncaster, she helped out at the family betting shop in the town centre.

Pat Baird was born in Longford in the Republic of Ireland and came from a broken home. After her divorce, his mother met a guy called George and they all moved over to Glasgow. Upon leaving school, Pat mixed with some colourful characters and worked as an on-course bookmaker.

Soon after Ian was born, the Bairds moved up to Glasgow, where they lived for almost a year. There was a further addition to the family with the birth of Ian's brother Darren. His youngest brother Gavin would come along some years later in 1974.

At the time, Glasgow offered very little and they were soon on the move again – this time to Southampton where, years previously, Pat Baird had worked on the cruise ship *Queen Mary*. Pat settled his family in an area of Southampton called Hedge End, where he found employment in the motor trade.

On the day Ian Baird was born, Southampton Football Club – for whom he would make his league debut as a raw 19 year-old – were involved in an extraordinary Second Division match at home to Derby County. Inspired by a Terry Paine hat-trick, the Saints beat their visitors 6-4. The game also proved to be Mick Hennigan's last appearance for the south coast club before a move to Brighton & Hove Albion. Hennigan would later work with Ian when employed as assistant manager to Howard Wilkinson at Leeds United.

Ian's younger days were very happy times; he was a chirpy little fella, always in good health. But at the age of six, there was a real cause for concern. During the summer of 1970, Pat decided to buy a property in Spain. He found a nice four-bedroom villa, for which he paid £3,000. The family travelled to Spain so Pat could sort out the necessaries and complete the purchase. It was on the return journey to England that Hilary noticed that Ian wasn't his usual self:

"On the way back, Ian was very quiet. I repeatedly asked him if he was alright and he would nod and tell me that he was fine. We arrived home on the Saturday evening and he went off to bed.

"During the night I woke to hear him whimpering, I checked on him and he was very restless. I informed Pat that something wasn't quite right, and at seven o'clock in the morning we called the Doctor. Ian was diagnosed, almost immediately, as suffering from meningitis."

Ian's parents were obviously distraught as he was rushed to hospital, where he would stay for a month. Hilary's side of the family had experienced a death due to the terrible illness, which very little was known about at that time. Thankfully, as Hilary explained, her eldest son battled his way to a full recovery:

"It really was a miracle that Ian came through. He was a strong, robust little character who never let the illness bother him. Teachers and friends from the school he attended were fantastic and proved to be a great help throughout his ordeal.

"In those days there were no televisions in the hospital, and when Ian's teacher Brother Bradley paid a visit, he would take a radio so they could listen to the football commentaries. Ian was a very popular little boy and his school-mates would send letters to him which all helped to keep his spirits up, and slowly but surely he battled back."

Just as Ian was ready to be discharged from the hospital, he contracted mumps and was forced to extend his stay by a further ten days. He was kept in isolation before being allowed to return home and back to his normal way of life.

There is no doubt that being able to listen to the football on the radio whilst in hospital did Ian a world of good. Although he enjoyed and excelled at many different sports, football was his main passion and his brother Darren would follow suit:

"Darren and I were besotted with football from an early age. Darren supported Leeds United and whilst we would be kicking a ball about in the garden, he would proudly wear the sock tags that Don Revie's team were famous for at the time. His tags sported the number seven, as worn by 'Hotshot' Lorimer, who years later I would play alongside at Elland Road."

Like all football fans, FA Cup Final day was a special occasion for the Baird brothers. At a time when televised games were a rarity, coverage of the final would start mid-morning. The cameras would follow the teams' coaches from the luxury surroundings of their hotels, through the masses of expectant fans on Wembley Way, all the way to the national stadium. Goals from previous rounds were broadcast, showing how the two clubs had battled their way to the season's showcase event. Interviews with managers and players, debate, opinion, and comedy moments provided hours of great television – all before a ball was even kicked. Ian and Darren would then go outside, into the garden, and 'replay' the game's key moments.

Ian's earliest memories of playing competitive football came with the local Scouts group, where he fancied himself as a goalkeeper. However, circumstances intervened and one day he was asked to play as a striker. He remained a centre-forward throughout a long professional career – other than one game for Heart of Midlothian in the Scottish Premier Division when, due to unforeseen circumstances, he played the whole game against Aberdeen between the sticks.

# 2

# Mischief and England caps

Ian was a typical boy who was never far away from any incidents and mischief. His Father Pat recalled one particular occasion which, although serious at the time, he now looks back on with some amusement:

"It was the middle of the night; Ian would have been around seven years old. He came wandering into our bedroom pissed out of his brains. He had woken up needing a drink, he went downstairs and drank liquid from a bottle thinking it was juice but he had in fact guzzled a load of sherry.

"The doctor rushed out but thankfully he didn't need medical attention and, typical of Ian, he was out playing football early that morning."

When Ian was nine, his parents' relationship hit a rough patch. Despite this, his childhood memories are extremely good ones:

"Mum moved us to Cheltenham for a short time and although they eventually patched things up and we returned to Hampshire, it was never the same. My parents always provided for us and we never wanted for anything. We lived in nice houses and had annual holidays down to Spain, where Dad owned the villa."

Ian's close friend Jeremy (Jerry) Hilton often travelled to Spain with the Baird family and on one particular holiday in the summer of 1976, Jerry had forgotten his passport:

"Hilary was taking Ian, Darren and I to the villa. We were ready to depart on the cross-channel ferry from Southampton, when I realised that I had left my passport at home. Fearing that I would have to be left behind, I laid myself down in the rear foot well behind the front seats. Ian and Darren covered me with a travel rug and sat with their feet resting on me. The ferry set sail and nobody had a clue that I was in the car.

"My mother flew to Spain with my passport later in the summer, to ensure that I would make the return journey with no concerns."

Once back in England and back at school, a budding young footballer was beginning to enjoy himself on the field of play:

"Having scored loads of goals for school teams and the Scouts, I progressed to play for the Hornets, a junior team managed by a lady called Mrs Gough who was brilliant with me.

"I then played for Sarisbury Sparks and then Bitterne Saints, both clubs were managed by a guy called Geoff Palmer. I played up front with Shaun McMenemy, the son of the Southampton manager, Lawrie – who would be stood on the touchline, watching his son and offering his encouragement.

"Lawrie obviously spotted some potential in me as at the age of 13, while studying at St Mary's, I signed schoolboy forms with the Saints.

"Darren was also playing football and Mum drove us here, there and everywhere. I turned out for various representative sides, from Southampton under-11s through to the under-15s, playing at one stage alongside Paul Rideout, culminating with trials for England Schoolboys."

Ian had no interest in academic subjects at school. He was at his happiest when kicking a football, competing in athletics or playing cricket in the summer. One of his classmates, Giles Watkins, remembers Ian's sporting achievements at a young age:

"The under-12s team which Ian played in won everything that year, the Southampton league and cup, along with the County Cup. I recall Ian being presented with a leather football in assembly after scoring in excess of 100 goals during the season. I wasn't quite good enough to play every game but I was often the substitute. I did start one game in which we won 13-0 with Baird scoring eight of them. He could find the net from practically any angle within reasonable distance.

"Ian was also a keen cricketer. He was a middle-order batsman and wicketkeeper. On one occasion he used my bat, a decent cricket bat made by Gunn and Moore. He hit this six and broke the handle. Unfortunately that piece of equipment was never quite the same.

"Another incident on the cricket field brought tears of laughter when, one summer's day, Ian in his role of wicket-keeper bent over to pick the ball up and split his trousers.

"Athletics was another sport which Ian excelled at. A rivalry built up between Ian and Chris Mitchell. During one particular school sports-day, Mitchell beat Ian over 100 metres and Trevor, Chris' father, went insane with pleasure. He was shouting how he'd waited four years to witness that. We were only 12 years old at the time."

Darren, although admitting that his elder brother was a pain in the arse as a kid, also admired Ian's sporting achievements:

"Ian was the best sportsman in the school, a real all-rounder. He was head and shoulders above everyone when it came to football and he scored goals for fun."

Away from school and the football field, Ian was a typical young lad who, along with a group of his mates, committed acts of mischief. Unfortunately, on two occasions, he was summoned to appear at Southampton Juvenile Court:

"By this time we lived in the Bassett area of Southampton, which like most places had mixed reputations. Although our house was deemed to be in the respectable area, I had mates, through playing for various football teams, who lived in the tricky part of Bassett.

"A lot of the time, particularly in the school holidays, boredom would set in and we'd often to get up to no good. The father of one of my mates, Alex Kickham, was a butcher on the ships and one day we got hold of his butcher's axes and chopped down a small tree on the estate where Alex lived. The incident was reported to Southampton Council, who called the police and we were prosecuted."

Alex Kickham remembers the police promising him that if he owned up it would not be taken any further:

"I duly admitted the offence but despite the original promise, Bairdy and I ended up in juvenile court, where Ian's dad told the judge that he should be lenient with us as the former US President George Washington had chopped a cherry tree down in his youth and he had turned out alright.

"We both received a stern warning about our future behaviour although Pat's comment caused some amusement afterwards, and for a short while his nickname for Ian was 'George Washington.'"

It was during his school years that Ian got his first job – working Sundays at Chilworth filling station, just a few miles from home. During one shift, which proved to be his last, Ian was asked to inflate the tyres on a customer's vehicle:

"A guy pulled onto the forecourt in one of those sky-blue-coloured disabled cars which were common back in the 1970s. The vehicle needed some air in the tyres, and somehow I managed to inflate the tyres to around 90lbs psi – basically around three times the amount of air required. When the guy drove away he almost killed himself and I received the sack."

The incident didn't deter Ian from trying his hand at various tasks if they would earn him a few quid, and Jerry Hilton remembers himself and Ian working for Pat Baird during the half-term holidays:

"Pat was kind enough to give us a job cleaning the cars. One day, he went off to the motor auctions so Ian and I thought it would be clever to go AWOL. We went into Southampton city centre to chase girls and look in the shops. However, we returned to the garage mid afternoon but Pat had got there before us.

"He went ballistic and to say he wasn't pleased is an understatement. He banned me from the place for a few months and sent me home to my parents.

"I spent a lot of time with the Bairds, and I was often the butt of practical jokes played by Ian and Pat. One night we were watching the television and I'd gone into the kitchen to get a drink and some food. When I returned to the living room, they had switched the television off, and were both sat laughing uncontrollably on the settee. Pat had placed a photograph of me on the top of the television set; it was one from school where I had the classic NHS spectacles on and one eye going in a different direction to the other due to a squint."

Around the late 1970s Ian and his mates started to take an interest in the opposite sex and one night, after a trip to the cinema, they found themselves in a spot of bother which Alex Kickham remembers well:

"Bairdy was dating a girl called Sandra O'Byrne and a group of us had gone to the cinema to watch a film. Afterwards a few of them boarded a bus to Bassett and I was sitting in the bus station, drinking a hot chocolate waiting for my bus.

"I suddenly noticed that the bus Bairdy was on was rocking from side to side. I looked up and could see that he was taking a beating by a group of lads who were a few years older than us.

"The bus driver had closed the doors and wouldn't let me on. I wanted to help my mate and managed to kick the doors open. He was having a good go but coming off worse due to the number of lads who had set about him. The driver had already called the Old Bill, and they soon arrived on the scene and restored order.

"That night Ian had been wearing a pair of dungarees and as he walked down the bus, one of the older lads called him 'John Boy' to which Bairdy turned around and told him to fuck off. And that's when the trouble started."

By now, Ian was making a huge impression in the Southampton area due to his ability on the football field. But when Pat eventually moved to Spain after a VAT problem with the Inland Revenue, Hilary was intent on moving the boys to her home town of Doncaster:

"When Dad went over to Spain it proved to be the final nail in the coffin as far as their marriage was concerned, and Mum wanted us to move up north. But I wasn't keen, mainly due to my football ambitions. Fair play to Mum, she agreed that we would remain in Southampton."

Ian realised one of his ambitions when, following trials, he won two caps representing England Schoolboys. The trials could not have come at a better time for Ian, as he was back in Southampton Juvenile Court with eight of his mates who faced 16 charges of breaking and entering:

"It was pure mischief and very stupid, but nobody got hurt. We would break into schools and kick footballs about, or we would break into social clubs and steal crates of beer. We got up to all sorts of nonsense and although we were summoned to court and we knew what we'd done was wrong, it was hardly on the scale of the Great Train Robbery."

The judge was lenient with Ian, having been told of his opportunity with the England Schoolboys, sending him for 20 hours in an attendance centre where he was given the 'short, sharp, shock':

"We would be made to run around the premises and do press-ups and sit-ups whilst some bloke barked orders at us. It wasn't the nicest experience in the world but I had to accept it as punishment for the mischief I got up to.

"Also, this is the first time that my dad will know about this, due to the fact that my mum managed to keep it from him. Sorry Dad!"

Ian soon realised that a life in football would be far better than a life of petty crime, and he set about proving his ability with the England Schoolboys.

Having been successful in the trials, Ian received the ultimate schoolboy footballer's accolade on Friday the 27th of April 1979, when he lined up for

England Schoolboys at Wrexham's Racecourse Ground. The opponents were Wales, with a team that included Mark Hughes, Clayton Blackmore and Mark Bowen, and young Baird played his part in a 2-1 win.

"It was tremendous to be picked for the England team. To be recognised as the best player in your position in the country was an unbelievable achievement and I was extremely proud."

A further cap followed against Scotland on Monday the 7th of May 1979, at St James' Park, Newcastle. The game ended in a 1-1 draw.

The 'pen pictures' in the match-day programme described Ian as having considerable experience with Southampton Schools FA and Hampshire County SFA. Also included in the England squad were Mike Hooper, Paul Rideout, Trevor Steven, Mark Walters and Darren Wood.

The Scotland squad included Bryan Gunn, David Bowman, Neale Cooper, Paul McStay, and two players who would later in life become Ian's team-mates: Russell Doig (at Leeds) and Gary Mackay (at Hearts).

Ian was also included in the next squad to face West Germany at Wembley. But an injury picked up in training the day before the game ruled him out, and that was that at international level. Though he later had trials with the England youth squad but did not get selected, nothing could dampen his enthusiasm:

"I was desperate to become a professional footballer, and on the domestic scene every scout in the South of England had been to watch me play. Paul Rideout and I were offered apprenticeships at Swindon Town. Paul signed but I elected to sign for Southampton, as they were on my doorstep."

# 3

# The apprentice

Ian left school to sign for the Saints with no academic qualifications; the exams he sat produced the dreadful results of one grade 'E' and five 'ungraded'. Some years later, Ian was the subject of a feature in the popular football magazine *'Shoot!'* When asked about qualifications gained at school, Ian claimed academic prowess with 8 'O' levels, telling the reporter who conducted the interview that he was the brightest in the family!

Southampton were renowned for their excellent youth policy and they boasted some good young players, Danny Wallace, Martin Foyle, Ian Juryeff, Steve Baker, George Lawrence, Eammon Collins, Timmy Cole, Barry Blankley, Ally Sperring, Russell Burtenshaw, David Poole, Jeremy Stagg and Dave Madden. The youngsters, all of whom Ian established lifelong bonds with, still enjoy 'reunions' to this day and reminisce about their early lives as apprentice footballers:

"It was a massive eye-opener joining Southampton, and you soon realised that you weren't as good or as quick as you thought you were. It wasn't easy either, we did the usual duties expected of a young footballer at the time – ground maintenance, cleaning the place and looking after the professionals' kit and boots.

"The staff at Southampton Football Club didn't just develop us as footballers, they taught us life skills and ensured we worked hard. The youth team competed in the Hampshire league and the opposition would look on us as being a bit flash, and every week we had the shit kicked out of us. However, this provided a very helpful insight into dealing with the situation if you were lucky enough and good enough to be thrust into men's football."

In addition to blooding the youngsters, McMenemy liked to have a few older heads around the place – and he pulled off a master-stroke in the summer of 1980, by signing two-time European Footballer of the Year Kevin Keegan from SV Hamburg. Ian, although he never played alongside Keegan, remembers the impact that the England international made at the club:

"Kevin was brilliant and gave the place a real lift. I suffered a broken ankle at a time when he himself was out with an ankle problem, and we did our rehabilitation together. Later on in my career while playing for Heart of Midlothian, we came up against his Newcastle United side in John Robertson's testimonial match. Kevin came into the dressing room, looking for me and passed on his best wishes. He is a fantastic guy who I have the upmost respect for."

Every apprentice wanted to work for Kevin. The eldest apprentice had the pick of the pro's, and he was well looked after as Ian recalls:

"Keegan gave his apprentice an additional £20 a week (we earned £16 a week back then), providing his boots, shoes and car were kept immaculately clean. He also provided bottles of aftershave which he received as a result of his advertising work with Brut."

Baird was given the job of working for midfielder Steve Williams:

"Steve was loud, brash, arrogant, and disliked by some. Despite this, we became good friends. He was very down to earth, there were no grey areas and you knew where you stood with him."

Back then the Saints trained at Wellington and on one occasion at the start of pre-season, McMenemy was doing a big speech to the playing staff – including the new apprentices. Ian had not packed Williams' slip and there was a tear in his shorts, Williams was furious and made his feelings known: "Who the fucking hell is my apprentice?"

When Ian held his hand up to make himself known, Williams boomed across the room, "Bring my kit like this again and I will kick you straight in the fucking bollocks."

Lew Chatterley was the assistant manager at The Dell, and he ensured the young lads were kept in line. He worked them hard and the experience is one that Ian hasn't forgotten.

"Nowadays you don't get away with dealing with and speaking to the young players in the manner that Lew did with us. I can still hear him shouting across the room,

'Where's that ugly bastard Baird? Go run me a bath and make sure the water is Mediterranean, nice and hot just how I like it'.

"After a while, I got pissed off with him and the abuse he was dishing out, I thought I'd give him some of his own medicine. I waited for the next order to run his bath and I filled it with scalding hot water. He put his foot in and went mental. Timmy Cole and I were some distance away with the vacuum cleaner on and could hear the screams. I apologised and took a real bollocking, but he never asked me to run another bath for him again.

"Another ticking off came my way while on laundry duty with Danny Wallace. We only had to take the laundry about 200 yards, but one day we were pissed off with it. Danny, not being the tallest, climbed in the laundry basket, I crawled under a table and we had a lie down for half an hour. Chatterley caught us. He went ballistic and gave us all the shit jobs for a full month, including cleaning the ground after home games. That was a job nobody liked as the place used to be filthy."

It was around this period that Ian embarked on his first business venture, along with pals Jerry Hilton and Alex Kickham. In all honesty it was a half-baked attempt to earn a few quid in the form of a 'company' called BHK Motors (Baird, Hilton, and Kickham). Alex was responsible for the administrative side:

"We would buy old part exchanges from a local dealer on Burlesdon Road, Sholing. After cleaning them up we would move them on – mainly through the motor auctions by Southampton Docks, where due to Pat's connections, we received a favourable commission rate. In the first month we sold on 33 cars.

"We incepted a Motor Trade insurance policy, which cost us £540. It was a ridiculous amount of money for us to pay and if we ever made any profit from the sale of vehicles, it was more luck than judgement.

"We endured a long hot summer and one particular female friend, who lived with her parents, had a swimming pool so when the opportunity came to spend the day with attractive girls round a pool, not much work was going to be done."

Jerry recalls an incident over some savings:

"Around that time, Ian and I decided to open a building-society account, and we would deposit £20 per week and use it to pay for holidays. Eventually we had a couple of grand sitting there, and a lad we 'employed' to help us valet the motors had bamboozled us into thinking he could invest our money and earn us incredible returns. Being young and greedy, we were taken in by him and he took us for the whole lot.

"Each time we asked where our money was, he continually lied about its whereabouts until one afternoon things came to a head. The lad had driven over to meet us and provide another excuse but unfortunately for him, he never got the chance. He parked the car, got out and – without a word being said – Bairdy landed a punch plum on his nose. It was a beauty and there was claret everywhere.

"Eventually, through Pat's help and negotiations with the lad's father, we got a little bit of our money back but we'd been taught a harsh lesson at a young age."

At the time of Ian's 18th birthday, his two-year apprenticeship with the Saints was coming to an end. The youngsters were all summoned, one by one, from the dressing room to McMenemy's office which was situated down the winding corridors within The Dell. Ian, believing in his own ability and desire to succeed, was confident that he would be among the lucky ones earning a contract, and not one of those who would be left picking up the pieces after they faced the harsh reality of being released:

"Just before it was my time to go and see Lawrie, my good friend and team-mate Timmy Cole emerged in tears, after learning he was to be released. However, I was confident of getting a deal."

Ian was not to be disappointed as McMenemy, a big commanding character who was raised in the North East, offered him a one year professional contract. In doing so, he told the promising centre-forward that he had done really well and he had a real chance of progressing in professional football with the Saints.

Having seen other lads such as Cole get released, Ian was delighted to receive the chance. The offer was on the table and he knew he had to do his best to take advantage of it:

"It was a fantastic opportunity, a place packed with full internationals and players that had played for England at under-21 level. Top-class footballers including Peter Shilton, Mick Mills, Steve Williams, Frank Worthington, David Armstrong, Nick Holmes and Steve Moran. I immediately thought to myself, how the hell do I get into the first team?"

# 4

## Breakthrough at Southampton

Ian worked hard and showed plenty of enthusiasm on the training ground. He was involved in the odd scuffle with Steve Williams and big Dave Watson. You had to be hungry and keen and the youngster showed that he was both.

It was much harder to make the breakthrough into the first team. At the time the manager could only have one substitute on the bench – unlike today, where naming seven options makes it far easier for clubs to introduce the younger players.

On the 15th of January 1983, Ian Baird took his first step towards a league football appearance when he was an unused substitute for a home game with Coventry City. The following month, on the 19th of February, he got his first taste of first team action at home to Sunderland, coming off the bench to replace Dave Puckett in the 21st minute.

Martin Foyle was set to be named substitute but the day before the game, in the final training session, he had taken a knock on his jaw. Ian was called up, despite showing indifferent form playing for the reserves.

Nick Holmes and Mick Mills scored in a 2-0 win making it a memorable debut:

"It was a dream come true, something I had worked hard to achieve. Dave Puckett had to come off after he had aggravated a hamstring injury and I was given my chance."

Baird didn't waste any time getting himself involved in the game. Within minutes he turned a Sunderland defender and made a determined run into the penalty area, only to be denied by a tackle from Gordon Chisholm. Soon after, a header had Chris Turner at full stretch and then in the 67th minute, Ian made a lasting impression when he put over a cross for Steve Moran, who laid the ball off for Mick Mills to score the second goal:

"I remember doing well. I got involved in the game and it should have been 3-0 when I knocked the ball down for Moran, but with the goal at his mercy he smashed a shot against the woodwork."

After the game, Lawrie McMenemy told the Southampton Echo, '*Ian Baird came on and made a very good debut. It was pleasing because I have watched the lad struggling to get his confidence back in the reserves and the 'A' team.*

'*There were five men and a dog frozen on the touchline when I watched Ian play in a Hampshire league match the other week and nothing was going right for him.*

'*If Martin Foyle had not aggravated an old jaw injury, I doubt whether Ian would have figured on Saturday but he took his chance well. He made a few mistakes but there was a lot of good there. Like the other two front men, he worked hard and unselfishly and it opened the way for the midfield boys to get the goals.*'

After his impressive 70-minute stint, Ian kept his place in the side and his full debut came the following weekend at Upton Park:

"The day before the West Ham United game, we were working on the set pieces on the training ground and that gave me a clear indication that I would be involved.

"I wore the number eight shirt at Upton Park and I was up against the experience of Billy Bonds and Alvin Martin who were fantastic players."

The game ended in a 1-1 draw after Danny Wallace had given Southampton the lead. Within five minutes of the opener Baird had the ball in the net but unfortunately, the diminutive Wallace was stood in an offside position and the referee, Maurice Robinson, disallowed the goal.

Although Baird was disappointed the goal did not stand, he knew once again that he had made an impact on the game and he was happy with his contribution:

"On the bus going home, Chris Nicholl told me I had done really well and there was me – a cocky youngster – thinking, this is it, I'm on my way now. It was a fantastic feeling to make my full debut for Southampton."

England legend Peter Shilton was in goal for Southampton for that game and he remembers a young Ian Baird coming through the ranks at The Dell:

"Ian was very confident and although he was still a kid, he played the game like a man. He had no fear, he gave his all whenever he got a chance and he never let the side down."

Having waited for his debut, the wait for his first league goal wasn't far away. It came in the following fixture, at home to Swansea City in front of 16,842 spectators. Ian remembers the goal, a victory, and a run-in with an experienced member of the opposition:

"I had got myself involved in the game and had seen a lot of the ball. My efforts paid off in the 63rd minute when I grabbed the equaliser, just two minutes after we had gone 1-0 down.

"Danny Wallace broke down the left wing and put a superb cross over, which I headed past Dai Davies at the near post. We went on to win the game 2-1, thanks to David Armstrong's winning goal.

"I also remember Leighton James, a fantastic player and Welsh International catching me late in a tackle. I got up and mouthed at him but straightaway I realised I was out of order.

"The facts of the matter were that although I was in awe of the lads I played with, I had no respect for any of the opposition. Reputations counted for nothing and all I wanted to do was play well, make a nuisance of myself on the field and be in the team the following week.

"It was an incredible feeling when I scored the first goal of my career. I hoped it would be the first of many to come. The next morning I was lying in bed with a cup of tea and the newspapers. There was I, splattered all over the sports pages. I thought that I ruled the world."

Another goal soon followed when Manchester City suffered a 4-1 thrashing at The Dell, a game in which Steve Moran scored a hat-trick. In the City side that day was Ivan Golac, who had recently moved to Maine Road from Southampton.

"We were 4-0 up just before half-time and Ivan went off injured. Steve Williams remarked that Golac had got the '4-0 illness' and wasn't interested. When Ivan was playing at The Dell, we used to call him 'King of the Gym', as when he was in there he thought he was the best footballer in the world."

Any parent would be so proud of their son making his mark in professional football and Pat was no different:

"We went to all the games, they were great days. Ian never failed to give 100% but, due to his determination and the way he played the game. I always had a fear he would get himself sent off. He took some stick on the pitch but he could certainly dish it out."

Martin Foyle who had come through the system with Ian remembers his team-mate for being a wind-up merchant and two people falling foul of his antics:

"One of the apprentices, Colin Dixon who came down from the North East, was late in for training one day. Bairdy told him that he had to sweep the main car park at the ground. The car park was huge and the poor lad was out there for the best part of the day and by the time he'd finished, in the corner of the car park, there was a little mountain of pebbles that he had swept up.

"Following one occasion when Bairdy had played for the first team, he had taken some stick from one of the other lads. At the end of the game, Bairdy phoned some of his mates and asked them to come down to the ground. It all ended when all four wheels were removed from the offender's car which was left on bricks."

Ian found himself back in the team early on in the 1983-84 season when Arsenal came to The Dell:

"Luckily I had stayed in the night before as I knew Steve Moran was struggling with an injury. He failed a fitness test on the morning of the game, and the gaffer told me just two hours before kick-off that I would be playing. The truth was that I wasn't feeling too well myself. I had a touch of the man-flu. However, I took to the field where I didn't have the best of games but I scored the only goal in a 1-0 win.

"After the game, I had a temperature of over 100, the physiotherapist checked me out and McMenemy went mental. I remember thinking, fucking hell – what have I got to do? He was right though, I shouldn't have played."

Ian's winning goal came in the 72$^{nd}$ minute, a simple tap in at the far post following some fantastic play by Danny Wallace.

# 5

# The 'loan' ranger

A few days after starting in a League Cup game against Carlisle United, Ian Baird was temporarily heading out of The Dell:

"I joined Len Ashurst's Cardiff City on loan, for three months. But going from Southampton, where I had everything done for me, into the rough and ready world of the Second Division was a real eye opener.

"I got on with things and I was happy that I had the chance to pay regular first team football. I didn't know anything about Cardiff City but I soon settled down to life in Wales.

"The club put me in digs and I was made to feel very welcome by Mrs Thorpe in Penarth, a town in the Vale of Glamorgan. She was superb and treated me like her son."

Ann Thorpe worked in the offices at Ninian Park and looked after a number of young players, including the Bennett brothers, Gary and Dave. Her own son Paul was himself a footballer, who went on to play for Yeovil Town for many seasons after being released by Bristol City. Paul is the same age as Ian and the two would socialise together on a regular basis.

Ian made his debut on the 19th of November in a 2-1 defeat at Oldham Athletic, and he scored his first goal for the Bluebirds on the 3rd of December in another defeat, this time against Brighton & Hove Albion at the Goldstone Ground:

"I did well at Cardiff City; I played 12 league games and scored six goals. In a strange coincidence, every goal I grabbed came away from home. The only time I did score at Ninian Park was in the Welsh Cup against Maesteg Park in front of a small crowd of just 905. Ironically, the opposing centre-half marking me was Paul Thorpe, the son of my landlady.

"Going to Wales was a great experience for me and thoroughly enjoyable. I played in a typically feisty derby game against Swansea and after one particular challenge, I required 14 stitches in a leg wound.

"The boss, Len Ashurst, was excellent. He was something of a legend in the game and along with his assistant, Jimmy Goodfellow; the pair filled me with confidence."

Despite being over in Wales, Ian still enjoyed returning to the south coast of England to socialise with his mates. He controlled it a bit more, but he was young and enjoyed the night life.

Centre-back Gary Bennett who went on to have a sound career with Sunderland was playing for Cardiff City at the time, and the two built up a good rapport:

"We became friends when Ian joined Cardiff on loan from Southampton – and like me, he was a young lad learning his trade. He was a great character to have around the place and he scored a few goals. You knew what you got with Ian and later on in my career when I had played against him, I always knew that I had been in a game."

One of Ian's favourite memories of his time at Cardiff City happened on the training ground:

"We were out there one day when John Toshack turned up and held a separate session for the strikers. There we were, running around in dirty, tatty training gear on a park covered in dog shit, and the Liverpool legend is giving us his invaluable advice. It was absolutely unbelievable, a real bizarre experience."

When the three-month loan spell was due to expire, Cardiff City made it known that they wanted Ian to stay. An offer was made to retain his services on a permanent basis. The bid was rejected, but had Southampton accepted the Welsh clubs offer, Ian admits he would have signed for the Bluebirds:

"I would have stayed, but Lawrie valued me at £100,000 and Cardiff could not raise that sort of money. The situation was out of my control but whilst I was there, I really benefited from playing regular football and it gave me confidence and belief that I could perform well and score goals.

"In addition, my time with Cardiff had put me into the spotlight and I had offers to go to other clubs. Denis Smith at York City came in for me, but me being me at that time thought, why the fucking hell would I want to play for York City?

"Manchester City and Billy McNeil were very interested and made enquiries (McNeil would come again later in my career when he managed Celtic), but I didn't even want to talk to him. Who did I think I was to ignore an approach from Manchester City? I was like George Best with no ability!

"Then on two occasions Middlesbrough declared their interest. But following discussions with their manager, Willie Maddren, I rejected their approaches."

It was a case of 'so near yet so far' for Southampton, who had reached the semi-final of the FA Cup before losing to Everton and finished the season as runners-up in the First Division title race. Some say they should have won the league, having finished just three points behind champions Liverpool.

By this point Lawrie McMenemy was becoming exasperated with his young front man, who was still not a regular in the side. Ian himself was beginning to have doubts about what he would do in life:

"I had six or seven months left on my contract and, in all honesty, I was becoming fed up with football. I questioned my desire to remain involved in the game. My brother Darren and my mate Jerry were working in the motor trade, and they earned more money than I did. Ridiculously I started to think, this isn't for me."

During the summer Lawrie McMenemy began to shape his squad for the new campaign. He let Frank Worthington, who was in the autumn of his career, go to Brighton & Hove Albion and Ian believed he would become a first team regular.

It wouldn't prove to be the case, as Lawrie's next move was to acquire the services of the experienced Scottish international striker Joe Jordan from Italian outfit Verona:

"I had stupidly presumed that I would be first choice and I was far from happy when Joe signed. Subsequently I went off the rails a bit, and Dave Madden, Timmy Cole, Jerry Hilton and I travelled down to Spain and stayed at my old man's villa.

"During the summer I did no training whatsoever; I did not do a stroke and on the day we reported back for pre-season training, we had to do a ten mile run. Not surprisingly I came in right at the back. Chatterley called me a party boy and gave me the biggest dressing down I had ever had. He was fuming and really laid into me. 'Who the fucking hell do you think you are, believing you can turn up at a First Division football club unfit just because you've had a sniff of a few games? You think you're Billy Big Time and don't have to do anything, you'll be lucky to have a league career the way you're going on'.

"I stood there looking at him and thought to myself, what the fuck is he going on about? He carried on shouting and finger pointing but I didn't take a blind bit of notice in what else he had to say."

As the season got underway, things did not improve and there was an incident during a night out after Southampton had beaten Norwich City in a league fixture at The Dell:

"Reuben Agboola had his drink spiked and trouble was brewing. Following a row with his missus he left the club, but when he got outside a mass fight broke out and Eammon Collins, Dennis Wise and I got involved, trying to help him out.

"Agboola ran out into the road and was hit by a car. This incident was reported to the club and it effectively finished his time at The Dell. We turned up on the Monday for training sporting black eyes, McMenemy understandably was far from best pleased, and I was well and truly on a downward spiral.

"Ironically Reuben was sold to Sunderland the following January and, five months later, they appointed Lawrie as their new manager and the pair were re-united."

Looking back, Ian admits his behaviour was stupid, his attitude was poor and he didn't do himself any favours:

"I was moaning to anybody that would listen about not playing week in, week out. But who was I to think that I had a divine right be in the team ahead of Joe Jordan? A player who had done the lot, he'd played for Scotland in World Cups and for Leeds United in a European Cup Final, he had played for top clubs in England and done very well over in Italy."

Joe admits he knew little of the young centre-forward, who was desperate to make an impact:

"After being out in Italy I didn't know anything about Ian Baird until I had worked with him at Southampton. The club had a great reputation for producing quality players and Ian was highly thought of. He did well when given a chance and he always displayed great determination on the field. But when he was out of the side, his attitude could sometimes let him down."

Ian grudgingly accepted that he wasn't going to be a regular in the starting line up, and went on the piss at every opportunity with Eammon Collins. After the morning training sessions, most afternoons were spent in the snooker club, *The Green Baize* – where more focus was put on beating his best break of 70 than on getting into the Southampton first team. Bizarrely, he still managed to do alright:

"I was named substitute here, substitute there, sometimes getting on, sometimes not getting on, starting one week, left out the next. But the stark reality of the situation was that I, being a young striker trying to make his way in the game, was never going to keep an experienced professional like Joe Jordan out of the team.

Whilst playing in the reserves, Ian soon began to realise that something had to change and a few words of wisdom came his way from Joe ,

"Joe was the ultimate pro, and he had the respect of everybody within the club – especially the young lads. He'd been in Italy and was way ahead of the rest of the playing staff and coaches with regards to the finer technical aspects of the game, such as the diets and expected fitness levels.

"Every day he would stay behind and do some extra training. The defining moment for me came when after one session; Joe took me to one side and told me a few home truths.

"In no uncertain terms, he informed me that due to the way I was behaving, I was not going to make it as a professional footballer. Also he knew that although I had not played too many games, I had picked up more bookings than any other player."

Joe had spotted some positive aspects of Ian's game and he knew that, if he could sort out his attitude and his off-the-field lifestyle, he had the necessary tools to become a good pro.

"Joe was everything that I wanted to be. I took his advice on board, and it was the kick up the arse that I had needed. I had let myself down and if it wasn't for the timely advice, I would have drifted away from a career in professional football."

From that point Ian really started to knuckle down and whenever Joe Jordan was unavailable, he got a place in the team – starting games at home to Queens Park Rangers and Chelsea, and away at West Bromwich

Albion. Although he did not score, the Saints were unbeaten in the three games.

David Armstrong, a key figure in the Southampton midfield, could see the qualities Ian possessed:

"He was a hard-working lad and Joe was a big influence on him, he learned some good habits from Joe and he made life very difficult for the opposition. Ian was confident and respectful to the senior pros, although he never gave them an easy time in practice games. He always showed he was determined and played with plenty of hunger and desire."

Ian was not involved on the 24th of November 1984, when Newcastle United came to The Dell. It was after the game that Lawrie McMenemy was talking with his opposite number Jack Charlton, and Ian Baird was pivotal to the conversation:

"That night Lawrie McMenemy phoned and told me he had been speaking to Big Jack, who was desperate for a centre-forward. The manager had recommended me and I would be joining Newcastle on loan."

Nick Holmes, Ian's team-mate at Southampton, admits Ian needed the loan moves and believes the experience gained from them was vital for his career:

"He was finding it tough to break into the first team and hold down a regular place. He worked hard and used his strengths; he was a trier with a bit of ability who wore his heart on his sleeve. Through that hard work, he fashioned himself a good career and I respect him for that."

The Newcastle side of that time included Peter Beardsley, Chris Waddle, John Anderson, Gary Megson, Wes Saunders, Pat Heard and Neil McDonald. Peter Haddock, who would become a team-mate of Ian's at Leeds United, was also at the club – along with a certain apprentice by the name of Paul Gascoigne.

Pat Heard and Gary Megson were residing in the same digs as Ian, and Pat remembers Ian's arrival at the football club:

"He was a big lad who took no prisoners. He was as brave as a lion, and he did reasonably well. We had some good individual players at Newcastle United but collectively we were struggling."

Ian reported for training having not met anybody involved with the club, and to his surprise there was no sign of the manager:

"I couldn't find Big Jack. So I introduced myself to his assistant, Ian McFaul, who informed me that the manager never turned up at the training ground until Thursday. When I eventually met Jack Charlton, he was dressed in a suit but sported a pair of wellington boots. He was a real character and apart from Beardsley and Waddle, he didn't know anyone else's name. He would call Wes Saunders 'Pat' and he referred to me as 'Phil'."

During that first training session, Ian took part in a practice match and he overheard Megson asking Chris Waddle, "Who the fucking hell is he?" and Waddle admitting he had no idea:

"Nobody had heard of me, but why would they have done? I was a young kid trying to make his way in the game, with a handful of appearances under my belt. These days, a young player makes the breakthrough, plays 10 Premier League games and the media want him in the England team."

Ian made his Newcastle debut just three days before Christmas, away at Aston Villa. But his old mate Paul Rideout would steal the headlines by scoring a hat-trick as Villa romped to a 4-0 win.

On Boxing Day Jack Charlton's side were back in the midlands, this time at West Bromwich Albion. Although Baird scored his one and only goal for his temporary employers in the 46th minute, they slipped to another defeat, this time by the odd goal in three.

Despite finding the net against the Baggies, Ian was dropped to the substitute's bench as Peter Beardsley returned to the side for the visit of Arsenal, who were inspired by Charlie Nicholas and took the points back south.

Next up was a North East derby against bitter rivals Sunderland, and Ian earned a recall due to an injury to Chris Waddle:

"I will always remember playing in that game as I wore the famous Newcastle number nine shirt. I was thinking, what the hell is going on here? There were almost 37,000 inside St James' Park, and we beat Sunderland 3-1. Beardsley produced an absolute master class and scored a hat-trick."

Chris Waddle admitted it was tough time for the club and, although Ian performed well when he played, Newcastle were finding it difficult:

"Collectively we weren't playing well during that period and although we had enjoyed a good start to the season, we were running out of steam. The one thing I remember about Bairdy was that he got booked every time he played for us!

"He was a good lad, and he was one of those players that you wanted on your side. There weren't many central defenders who looked forward to playing against him; they knew they would be in for a tough afternoon. It didn't matter if they were established internationals or young lads that were marking Ian Baird; he would treat them all the same and give them a rough ride. Reputations counted for nothing."

Ian became good friends with Neil McDonald and had some good nights out. After one of the those nights, Ian smashed his car up the following day on the way back to Southampton, and acknowledges he was very lucky to get away with the incident.

Ian's temporary spell at St James' Park ended in a similar fashion to the way it began when, in his final appearance, the side suffered a 4-0 defeat away from home. This time at Goodison Park, at the hands of Everton.

Despite being booked in each of his five appearances and scoring just the one goal, Ian enjoyed his brief stint in the North East and was desperate to stay at Newcastle. But for one reason or another, the deal didn't happen. So, it was back to The Dell, back to the reserves, and back to his old ways:

"One Saturday night we had been out drinking and I decided to drive home. It was common in them days, look at the number of footballers that were done for drinking and driving. However, it was stupid and there was no excuse, but that was me at the time. We were in my motor and two of my mates were stood up in the back with their heads out of the sun roof, shouting at everybody as I drove through Southampton city centre. Out of nowhere came the sirens and blue lights – the Old Bill were chasing me through the streets. I turned into a side road, got out of the car and ran into a restaurant that I was a regular visitor to, it was run by an Israelite called Noah. I hid under a table but the diners pointed me out as soon as the police came charging in.

"Needless to say, they carted me off and I spent an uncomfortable night in the cells. I was planning on keeping it a secret from my dad because I was shit-scared of him and what he'd say. I even told the Old Bill my name was Jerry Hilton!

"That plan obviously failed, and I realised there was no chance at all of keeping it quiet. The news was all over Radio Solent and the local paper, leaving my old man and Lawrie McMenemy not best pleased to say the least."

After playing on a regular basis at Cardiff City and Newcastle United, Ian was confident that he could more than hold his own; he knew he lacked pace, but he also knew that he had enough about him to become a good footballer.

It wasn't until February that he started another game for Southampton's first team. Joe Jordan was set to serve a two match ban, and missed the game against Nottingham Forest at the City Ground. Ian started and although Southampton lost 2-0, he kept his place the following week, at home to West Bromwich Albion on the 2nd of March. Ian's only senior goal that season had been for Newcastle against the same opposition and this time he went one better:

"I managed to score two goals in two minutes at the start of the second half, they were both headers. George Lawrence provided the first cross and David Armstrong the second."

The Saints won the game 4-3 and Ian became the first Southampton player to score two goals in his final appearance for the club, as soon afterwards it came clear that he would never wear the red and white shirt again.

# 6

## Marching on Together

Eddie Gray was on the look-out for a striker and Ian's ability had been brought to his attention. The Leeds United manager had a few targets, but was hampered by the club's almost desperate financial situation.

Gray's assistant, Jimmy Lumsden, and chief scout Tony Fawthrop travelled to watch Ian play for Southampton reserves. They liked what they saw and a bid of £75,000 was accepted. The fee was made up of £50,000 up front and then a further £25,000 after 20 first team appearances.

Tony Fawthrop remembers seeing a deal for Leeds to sign Kerry Dixon from Reading fall through before attention was turned to Ian Baird:

"We drove down to Hampshire and came away well before the end of the game. I rang Eddie and told him that we should sign Ian. He proved to be a very good signing for Leeds United and he was just what we needed at the time. He was a great kid and a very good player."

Despite selling Baird, Lawrie McMenemy held him in high regard. He fully understood that the young striker needed to be playing first team football and he knew the move would be good for Ian:

"I had spotted Ian many years before, playing for Sarisbury Sparks. My son Shaun played in the same team and they formed a good partnership up front. I rated Ian, but there were some fantastic strikers at the club and his chances were limited. With only one substitute in those days it was much more difficult to give your squad players and youth players time on the pitch, and Ian needed to be playing. I was pleased he went on to have a good career, he was a hard-working lad and he was a very strong character."

After turning down Middlesbrough in the past and not wanting to speak to Manchester City, Ian felt he couldn't let the chance to join Leeds United slip by. He admits he didn't even know where the Yorkshire side were in the league table, but following another conversation with Joe Jordan – who had enjoyed much success in his time at Elland Road in the 1970s – Ian was convinced that it would be a great move for him:

"I knew deep down that I had no long-term future at Southampton, and if I wanted to fulfil my ambitions I had to move on. Joe told me that Leeds was a fantastic club and, although they had fallen on hard times in the old Second Division, it would be an opportunity I couldn't turn down."

As a result of the drink-drive conviction, Pat drove his son up to Elland Road on the Sunday morning where Eddie Gray was patiently waiting:

"I met Eddie at the ground and we had a long chat. I was very impressed by what he had to say, although he didn't need to sell the club to me. I wanted to be there."

Ian signed a two-year contract on £300 per week and £50 appearance money. The club put him up in the Dragonara Hotel and the following morning, before training, he was introduced to his new team-mates. Leeds had a very young squad at the time – John Sheridan, Tommy Wright, Denis Irwin, Scott Sellars, Neil Aspin and Terry Phelan, mixed with the experience of Peter Lorimer, Mervyn Day, Gary Hamson and Frankie Gray.

Tony Fawthrop recalls the new striker asking Eddie, prior to his first training session, if he should go easy on his new team mates – and it didn't take long for Baird to make an impression:

"We had a practice game in training on the Monday and I partnered Andy Ritchie up front. I did enough to impress Eddie, who put me straight into the side for my debut the following night away at Portsmouth.

"It was cold and wet, and when I ran out onto the pitch at Fratton Park I was amazed at the vast amount of Leeds fans in the ground. Straightaway I knew that I had made the right move."

Portsmouth were challenging for promotion and won the encounter 3-1, but Leeds felt they should have taken something from the game. Frankie Gray had the ball in the net but the referee disallowed the goal and awarded a penalty due to the fact that the debutant, Baird, had been fouled in the build-up.

The usually reliable Peter Lorimer missed the spot kick and, although John Sheridan netted from the rebound, 'Lash' would miss another penalty later in the game:

"I saw enough of my new team-mates to know that they were decent players. I immediately felt at home. The difference between Leeds and Southampton, without being disrespectful to Southampton, was massive in terms of the fans' intensity and the way they got behind you. It was something else at Leeds."

It was a proud moment for Darren, seeing his older brother sign for the club that he had supported since he was a boy:

"It was amazing. I travelled everywhere with my mates from Southampton to watch Leeds. We would often go in the South Stand at Elland Road, and to see my brother wearing the white shirt and scoring goals was unbelievable, and I was obviously very proud."

Hilary, Ian's mum, wasn't initially so keen on the idea of her eldest son moving north, and although it worked out well there was a tinge of sadness:

"I told Lawrie McMenemy that he had no right or reason to send my son all the way to Leeds. In the end it worked out so well for Ian and the Leeds United supporters loved him. But I do have one regret, in that my father was a Leeds fan but he had passed away before Ian played for them. He would have been so proud to have seen his grandson play for the club he loved."

Ian's home debut came on the 16th of March, in a Yorkshire derby against Barnsley. Eddie Gray wrote in his programme notes:

'*Hopefully, matters will now improve in the above respect (lack of goals) with the arrival of Ian Baird from Southampton. Ian is the type of player I have been seeking for some time now to introduce further options up-front and I am sure he will enjoy a fine career at Elland Road.*'

Baird hit the ground running at his new club and made goals for Lorimer and Sellars on his home debut. But just two weeks into his Leeds career he was up in front of a FA disciplinary committee at Brammall Lane, Sheffield – after picking up a stack of bookings, mainly in the reserves at Southampton and on loan at Newcastle. In addition, he was booked in each of his first two appearances for Leeds.

Having already served two suspensions earlier in the season, Ian was asked to explain his total of 41 disciplinary points.

The booking against Barnsley, for a challenge on defender Joe Joyce, was his 12th of the season and Eddie Gray believed Baird had become a victim of his own determination to succeed. The Scot accompanied his new striker on the trip to meet the football authorities, which resulted in Ian receiving the expected punishment:

"I was fined £200 and banned for two matches, which meant I missed games away at Fulham and at home to Blackburn Rovers. In the 10 games I played before the end of the season, I scored six goals. The first of which came away at promotion-chasing Manchester City in front of a 33,553 crowd on Easter Monday, a game we won 2-1.

"I equalised with a header when Lash put a great ball over, and I got up above Nicky Reid to head in at the far post before Scott Sellars bagged the winner.

"It was the first time in my career that I had come up against Mick McCarthy. Mick was a tough man and a no-nonsense centre-half. For 90 minutes he was trying to smash me all over the place and I was trying to smash him all over the place, it was a great battle."

The game was littered with bookings and wasn't short of incident. Ian picked up another yellow card and Manchester City's Graham Baker suffered a broken leg following a 50-50 challenge with Neil Aspin.

It was a welcome return to action for the new man following his suspension. The result surprised many and left 5,000 Leeds fans ecstatic at the final whistle. The start Ian made to his Leeds career and the way the fans took to him filled him with confidence, and he soon began to understand what was required on a personal level:

"I began to realise how I could make a serious living out of professional football. I needed to improve my first touch, improve my heading ability and put myself about even more. I hated the opposition and wanted to frighten the life out of them, always giving one hundred per cent with a desperate urge to win the game. I felt honoured that Eddie Gray had wanted to sign me. The man is an absolute legend, look at the career he'd enjoyed as a player."

Pictures of the great Leeds sides of the 1960s and 70s dominated the walls of the reception at Elland Road, and there was always a good atmosphere in the players' bar:

"We would be in there after a game, and the likes of Norman Hunter and Allan Clarke would come walking in. Bearing in mind that I had been brought up watching these players on television, it was unbelievable. I realised how lucky I was to be playing for Leeds United – who were a much bigger club than Southampton, even though they were in a lower division. The fans followed us everywhere in their numbers, and they were fantastic to me."

Ian quickly adapted to northern life and it was soon a case of play hard, work harder:

"Training was enjoyable. Shez was always giving Peter Lorimer stick and often called him 'sponge nose'. We were cocky young lads, full of confidence, and both Eddie Gray and Jimmy Lumsden were fantastic to us. They gave me a huge lift and they both believed in me. No disrespect to Lawrie McMenemy, who was a brilliant manager, but his main strengths were with older, more senior professionals.

"There were a few strikers at Leeds when I joined and I enjoyed working with them. They all had different strengths and qualities and were all great lads. Scotsman George McCluskey had arrived from Celtic where he had scored plenty of goals, and although things didn't really work out for him at Elland Road, he had his moments. A goal he scored at Shrewsbury Town lives long in my memory and some of the things he did on the training ground were unbelievable.

"Andy Ritchie was a top player but he was the tightest footballer you will ever meet. He would join in the card school at the back of the bus, win a few hands, take the money and fuck off back down the front.

"Then there was Tommy Wright, a youngster from Scotland, a great little footballer with an eye for goal. But his Leeds career would come to an end mainly due to a misdiagnosed injury."

Assistant manager Jimmy Lumsden soon recognised the qualities that Baird had in his locker, and many years later he tried to sign him whilst managing Bristol City:

"Ian was a great lad. It's a shame we didn't bring him in at Christmas and had we done so, I firmly believe we would have got promoted. We had some good strikers at the club but Bairdy gave us something else. He gave us an extra edge and he settled in well, impressing everybody."

Leeds United went into the last game of the season, away at Birmingham City, with an outside chance of going up. Birmingham were also in the thick of the promotion race and the ground was packed, Leeds fans were everywhere and the atmosphere was horrible:

"The lads knew there would be problems. We had been told that there had been some trouble on the Friday night, and as we were travelling to the ground we drove past some wasteland and there was fighting going on there."

"Before the game started, the police came into the dressing room and instructed that if we did score then under no circumstances do we run towards our own fans to celebrate. They knew they had a serious situation on their hands and were starting to panic."

The game got underway but when Martin Kuhl gave Birmingham the lead just before half-time, all hell broke loose and Ian remembers the unsavoury incidents.

"The referee stopped the game and asked Eddie to go over to the Leeds fans and try to calm them down.

"The match was delayed and during this time the Leeds directors offered to concede the game. After 35 minutes, play restarted but when the game eventually ended, so did our slim promotion hopes due to a 1-0 defeat. As fans spilled onto the pitch at full time, Mervyn Day and Gary Hamson were attacked as we frantically tried to make our way to the security of the dressing rooms."

Football paled into insignificance soon after when a 12-foot wall by the directors' car park behind the main stand collapsed and a teenager, who was attending his first ever game, tragically died from his injuries.

A total of 176 people were injured during the day's catastrophic events and as a result of the violence, the police made 125 arrests. The players were locked in the ground for two hours, and that was when they began to hear about the tragic fire at Valley Parade:

"As we boarded the coach, the radio was broadcasting news from Bradford and we could not believe what we were hearing. Normally Lash, Frankie Gray and George McCluskey would be on the coach enjoying the odd whisky while the younger lads would be playing brag. On this occasion, there was nothing but stunned silence.

"It was a truly sad day and the events which unfolded at Birmingham and Bradford were, and still are, difficult to understand."

# 7

## Tears at the Flying Pizza

By the summer of 1985, Ian's relationship with Lesley Lowman had blossomed The couple had known each other since their schooldays, and first dated in December 1984.

Ian had purchased a house in Thorpe Hesley, a suburb of Rotherham – and Lesley left her parents' home and moved up north to be with him.

During the build up to the big kick-off, Leeds were banned from travelling on any continental pre-season tours following the carnage at St Andrews and all friendlies had to be arranged in England.

The bookies had installed Leeds as favourites for promotion and Ian was raring to go:

"I'd been on holiday to Spain and although I had done some running during the second week, it did not prepare me for what was in store when we returned to Fullerton Park.

"Eddie and his coaching staff absolutely mullered us. It was the hardest pre-season programme I had ever been put through. We did well in the friendly matches and we were really confident going into the new season."

The season started at Craven Cottage against Fulham. Ian partnered George McCluskey up front and Leeds took an early lead through Peter Lorimer:

"I thought, here we go, we're up and running. But we ended up losing 3-1. We probably deserved better on the day, although Fulham had a decent young side which included Ray Houghton and Paul Parker."

Ian Snodin had joined in the summer from Doncaster Rovers for a £200,000 fee. Leeds had managed to beat off strong competition from West Bromwich Albion and although both Sheffield clubs made late bids, the much sought-after midfielder decided to move to Elland Road. The two Ians soon became good mates:

"Snod was a class act and the fastest thing on two legs you've ever seen. I built up a great friendship with him and he would drive me in to training every day. I was still banned, and had been catching a bus to Chapeltown on the outskirts of Sheffield and then a train into Leeds. Ian would go 45 minutes out of his way to pick me up and would never take any petrol money, he was a great lad. His family are good people who are down to earth and would do anything for you.

"During the time we played at Leeds together, we had some memorable journeys into training. One particular morning David Harle was driving us in, he'd picked Snod up first and on the way to collect me, a stone had hit his windscreen and shattered it. It was the middle of winter and it was freezing cold. They arrived at my house and had planned on going in my car but Lesley had already gone to work in it.

"Harley somehow decided it would be a good idea to use a hammer and smash the whole windscreen through. He then asked for a carrier bag, which he put over his head. He made holes in it so he could see and secured it round his neck with Sellotape before setting off on the journey to Leeds.

"He was flying down the M1 in the outside lane with me and Snod huddled under a coat on the back seat. It was absolutely freezing. We got to Leeds and Dave couldn't get his hands off the steering wheel, they were frozen to it and there was ice on his eyes. He got in the warmth of the dressing room but it took him an hour to thaw out.

"Another time Ian had bought a new motor, a Mitsubishi Colt, and one morning he picked me up with John Buckley also in the car. On the motorway, and a fair distance from Leeds, the temperature gauge was going up and up but he ignored it and carried on driving.

"Eventually, he decided to pull over into a slip road. He lifted the bonnet and unscrewed the cap. Instantly, steaming hot water blew out all over his face. We were trying to flag down a car for some help, his face was practically on fire and he was shouting for somebody to get him a flannel.

"Luckily there was a police car not far away. We jumped in and got a lift to Barnsley hospital, with Buckley and I sat in the back pissing ourselves laughing. All we could hear was Snod, still shouting that he wanted a flannel.

"After spending a few days in the hospital, he returned to Elland Road to find that the lads had put a sign on the dressing room door which read, 'Get me a flannel'. When he walked into the dressing room, he saw a load of flannels hanging on his peg with another sign – 'You wanted a flannel, we've got you a fucking flannel!'

"Soon after moving into my house, I bought a little German Shepherd who I called 'Rocky'. Snod picked me up in a brand new white XR3i and he didn't mind when I asked him if I could bring the dog.

"We arrived at the ground and while we were training I left the dog in the car. We returned later to discover that he had chewed the seats and the headrests, there was hardly anything left of the interior. Ian brushed it aside, saying it was one of them things. I would have been fuming.

"On the odd occasion we would drive in to training wearing bobble hats and daft glasses. We would be in the back seats licking the car windows. People driving past would often toot their horns and make gestures to us. It was daft things but we had some laughs."

Leeds really struggled to get going after the defeat at Fulham and it wasn't until the 4th of September that they picked up their first win of the season, a 1-0 victory away at Brighton & Hove Albion. During the bad run, they reached a real low point when they were hammered 6-2 at Stoke City in a game that was all square with less than 20 minutes to go:

"We were very disappointed; we went in 1-0 down at the interval and were very much in the game. Unfortunately after drawing level from 2-0 down, we inexplicably caved in."

The manager, Eddie Gray, who publicly described the performance as 'disgraceful', admitted that anxiety had crept into their play and Ian admits that his manager was understandably far from happy:

"The boss read the riot act the following day. Most of the lads had never been in that type of situation. But instead of things improving, they got worse. We couldn't handle the 'favourites' tag and the expectation. Eddie and Jimmy were on edge and they didn't seem themselves. The pressure was mounting, everybody began to feel it and arguments were a regular thing within the camp. Shez and I had words during the thrashing at Stoke City and we didn't speak for three weeks. We were both headstrong and didn't want to break the silence, but eventually I backed down and we sorted things out."

John Sheridan remembers the incident well:

"Bairdy came into the dressing room at half-time and fronted me. In an attempt to avoid him cracking me, I picked a boot up. Words were exchanged and we didn't speak for a while. But these little fall-outs often happened, it was part and parcel. It showed the frustration and the passion we both shared."

The whole team was struggling, and Ian admits that his own form was poor and he wasn't playing well:

"We played a local derby at Huddersfield on the 5th of October and although I scored, Shez was sent off and we lost 3-1. The supporters weren't happy and were starting to turn on us. I went out in Doncaster that night with Snod and a few other lads, and a group of Leeds fans were demanding answers as to what was going on."

The following game saw the Whites progress in the League Cup after winning 3-0 at Walsall, and the feeling was that a corner had been turned. But nobody could have imagined what was to happen next:

"After being given the day off after the game, we went into training on the Thursday morning. Peter Gunby came over and his words knocked me for six. 'They've sacked Eddie, they've fucking sacked him. Get in there and see the chairman.'

"Ian Snodin and I went in to see Leslie Silver, but he completely dismissed what we had to say. I imagined him thinking, 'I am a multi-millionaire businessman and these two scrotes are telling me how to run my football club'.

"Peter Gunby, who was a great bloke, took temporary charge but training was a complete waste of time. Lash did his best to lift the spirits but there was no atmosphere, the lads were devastated. We all went to see Eddie and Jimmy later that day. They were in the Flying Pizza and most of the young lads were in tears, me included. He was like a surrogate father and we couldn't believe the situation we had found ourselves in."

Andy Ritchie echoed the feelings of the squad:

"It was a shock and a huge disappointment. Eddie was liked by everybody, he was a real legend."

On the Saturday Leeds played Middlesbrough at Elland Road, and won the game 1-0 courtesy of a Peter Lorimer penalty. It was a spot kick that the club's all-time top goalscorer contemplated missing in protest at Eddie's dismissal. However, he did the right thing and put the ball into the net for the only goal of the game.

There was unrest all afternoon – fans demonstrated before, during and after the game. It was all aimed at Leslie Silver and his board of directors. Eddie was very popular amongst the supporters who showed their feelings that afternoon.

Just two days later, Leeds played in the Full Members Cup, a new and meaningless competition which never caught the fans' imagination. On that night at Maine Road against Manchester City, there were less than 5,000 supporters in the ground:

"We were riled on the coach to Maine Road when Leslie Silver told us that Eddie has gone and life moves on. He said it in a cocky manner and it didn't go down very well to say the least. One of the lads shouted out, 'Who the fucking hell is he?'

"Not one of us on that coach wanted to play that night and in reality we didn't. We got trounced 6-1."

Included in the Leeds squad was young Welsh striker Lyndon Simmonds, who was set to make only his second appearance for the club, and his first that season:

"I should have been thrilled. But honestly that night, I wasn't. I was sub, City were battering us, the lads weren't interested and I didn't want to come on. The players felt that Eddie had been stabbed in the back. It was fair to say that the whole evening was a truly horrendous experience."

# 8

# Bremner, Warner & Cheeseboards

There was the usual speculation in the media as to who would replace Eddie. Every Tom, Dick and Harry was being touted for the job. But the board made a relatively quick appointment, and installed former captain Billy Bremner as manager.

Billy took charge of Leeds for the first time on the 27th of October, at Barnsley. But despite playing well for long periods and hitting the woodwork a couple of times, Leeds were far too generous at the back and lost 3-0 in what had become a familiar story:

"That was the way things were at that time. Snod assured me all would be well, he and Billy knew each other inside-out from their time together at Doncaster Rovers.

"Bremner was fantastic with us and he really looked after us. He was a true Leeds United legend who loved everything about the club he had captained to glory throughout his playing career.

"He was such an infectious guy, after training we would sit and listen to the stories he told us of the great Leeds side he played in. Quite often we would be there for up to two hours, he loved it and so did we. The stories would continue on the coach to and from away games, Billy would sit there playing cards, smoking a fag, reminiscing about the club's heady days under Don Revie."

Ian was a real favourite of Billy's, and Andy Ritchie recalls an incident one particular Monday after training:

"We'd been beaten on the Saturday, and Billy had held a team meeting after Monday's training session. He told each and every one of us what he thought of the individual performances and he really dished out some bollockings. When he came to Bairdy, Billy praised him, saying he'd covered every blade of grass over the 90 minutes. I nicknamed him the 'Hover Mower'. He was like the teacher's pet, Billy adored Ian."

Having seen it and done it with 'Super Leeds', it was clear that Billy often got frustrated at times. On the training ground he was no longer out there with the likes of Johnny Giles, Paul Madeley, Paul Reaney and Allan Clarke; he was dealing with a mixture of journeyman footballers and young lads trying to establish themselves in the game. It was a transitional period, Leeds were struggling at the wrong end of the league, and Baird concedes that it was a really frustrating time for the club:

"The performances were inconsistent; we would win one game then lose two. I was sent off at Wimbledon after scoring the second goal in a 3-0 win. It left me very disappointed as I had just got back into the side having served a three-match ban. We had been on the back foot, and had Mervyn Day to thank when he saved a first half penalty. Then, just before half-time, Snod scored before I made it 2-0 soon after. Martin Dickinson made it 3-0 and we were cruising. Stupidly, late in the game I got involved in an off-the-ball incident with Andy Thorn, and the referee sent me off after consulting one of his linesmen.

"We won the following week and then lost three on the trot. We could not get going with any major momentum. But eventually one or two signings came in, and we climbed away from the danger zone."

Many of Eddie's young team were departing the club. Billy Bremner had his own ideas and wanted his own personnel. Defender Brendan Ormsby, who would be made captain, arrived from Aston Villa after Dave Rennie had been recruited from Leicester City. The pair helped steady the ship and played a big part as Bremner's men won four of the last seven games, ensuring that Leeds would be playing Second Division football the following season.

"We did well towards the end of the season but, after we lost at Crystal Palace 3-0 in April, there were fans waiting for us when we got back to Elland Road and we took some abuse. It had been a poor performance and we knew it."

The final game of the season saw Leeds travel to East Anglia to play Norwich City. The Canaries had been crowned Champions and they were presented with the trophy. As they paraded it to the supporters on the traditional lap of honour, Billy told his players that next season it would be them:

"We believed him, we trusted his every word. He was superb with us and was very much a father figure, similar to how Eddie Gray had been. If we'd had a few beers on the coach on the way home, he would take our car keys from us and give us the money for a taxi. He tried to guide us in life as well as football. This was evident when in the end Billy banned the card school. Shez and I lost our wages on a few occasions and we started to take it personally but Billy wouldn't let that continue."

One particular character, first introduced to the club by Jack Charlton when Don Revie was appointed manager, was brought back by Billy and he helped to raise the spirits within the camp.

Scotsman Herbert Warner was a Jewish jeweller who lived in north Leeds. He socialised with Jack Charlton, who introduced him to The Don.

Anthony Clavane's much acclaimed book, 'The Promised Land', acknowledges that Don felt comfortable in the company of members of the Jewish community – and when he met Herbert, the foundations of a great friendship had been laid. Herbie, as he was known, would become a big part of Don's inner circle as the Whites enjoyed great success at home and abroad.

Herbie was a wheeler and dealer, an entertainer and a very infectious personality. He would tell jokes to the players and relax the squad before games. Carpet bowls, bingo and dominoes were all arranged by Herbie, and he would organise the players' social lives.

Dave Cocker, the son of the legendary trainer Les Cocker, remembers Herbie well:

"He became the punch-bag for dressing room banter and the players, especially Billy, used to rib him constantly. They would show no mercy but Herbie would take it all on the chin.

"On one particular European away trip, Billy entered Herbie's hotel room whilst he was sleeping and nicked his false teeth, his glass eye and his wig. He had to endure the whole trip minus these items, and it was only on the approach to Leeds/Bradford Airport that he had them returned. The lads were throwing his wig around the plane, and after that incident he never wore it again.

"Another memorable occasion occurred before a domestic away game. Bets were placed on a race before kick-off between Herbie and Jim Lister. Jim was the bus driver and both blokes were unfit, similar build and overweight. The two of them were to run from the halfway line to the goal. After 15 yards, they were both walking and the supporters inside the ground had no idea what was going on."

Baird also retains fond memories of Herbie:

"Herbie was a real character; he had a glass eye, false teeth, a bald head and a big nose. He was dripping in jewellery and he must have owned more gold than Mr T.

"The lads used to hammer Herbie, on a regular basis he would get thrown in the bath or his bald head would be drawn on with marker pens. He was good fun and would arrange games of carpet bowls and bingo. Shez would run a book and the lads loved it.

"Herbie would come on the training ground and try and kick the ball. He was useless at football and he would fall over in the mud and his clothes would be filthy. He always wore white shoes, white trousers and pink jumpers.

"Howard Wilkinson was appointed as manager. His first game in charge was away from home. We were on the team bus waiting to embark on the journey, when Wilko spotted Herbie sitting amongst the players. He asked him who he was and why he was there. Herbie responded telling the new manager that he was the club comedian. Wilko told him in a very abrupt manner that he wasn't welcome as there were enough comedians on the playing staff. That was the end of Herbert at Elland Road and unfortunately he passed away a couple of years later.

"We enjoyed some great times under Billy and the dressing room was a good place to be. John 'Nobby' Stiles would take the piss out of me and all the lads with his impersonations. He was a great lad, was John, but he was always moaning he had no money and his appearance was dreadful. You wouldn't have seen Steptoe in some of the clothes he wore.

"Some people looked on the lads that Billy brought in as being bad signings, but in truth they weren't bad signings. The harsh facts were that Leeds United didn't have a pot to piss in, and Billy put his trust in some of the lads that had played for him and served him well at Doncaster Rovers.

"Brian Caswell was permanently injured, he was very unlucky. David Harle got in the side and then suffered a bad injury. John Buckley was another lad who always seemed to be on the treatment table. He scored the winner against Reading before the bad luck set in. They were good lads, but through no fault of their own it just didn't happen for them at Leeds.

"Harley was a real character. He was rough and tough, he dressed like Tom Jones and he was brilliant for the dressing room banter and a laugh a minute on nights out.

"A load of us, one night, went out in Sheffield. We were in the popular night club *Josephine's*, and Harley and a few more turned up having paid a visit to the imaginatively named establishment, *Birds of Paradise*. Harley was rather disgruntled and proceeded to explain to us that he'd had a run-in with the management. The reason was, he claimed the madam had failed to satisfy him and he became embroiled in a blazing row as he demanded his money back."

Another character was John Stiles, and he recalls a few incidents involving Baird and goalkeeper Mervyn Day:

"In training we were doing some leapfrog exercises, and Bairdy was knelt down waiting for Merv to leapfrog him. However, Merv didn't seem to know what was happening. He put his hands behind his back and tried to jump over Ian from a standing position. He didn't manage it and fell over Bairdy head first, he landed flat on his face on the ground and smashed his nose all over the place.

"Whenever we travelled to an away game I would take the piss out of Merv at the dinner table and the way he ate his food. Bairdy would be crying with laughter and then when it was time to order the desserts, all the lads would choose ice cream and gateaux whilst Merv, who is a bit of an aristocrat, would ask to see the cheeseboard.

"He would be ridiculed for it time and time again, but Bairdy informed me on one trip that he was going to be like Merv and enjoy a bit of cheese.

"Sure enough, we were in the dining room and Merv made his usual request and ordered a bit of Brie and some Stilton. When the waiter approached Bairdy for his choice of desert, he turned to him and asked in a posh voice, 'Have you got any facking Cheddar?' It left Merv far from impressed and the rest of the lads were in stitches."

# 9

# The glorious failures

As Leeds United prepared for the 1986-87 campaign, manager Billy Bremner had signed the prolific striker Keith Edwards from Sheffield United – hoping the man from the Steel City could fire the Whites to the First Division.

It was a move that never really worked out for Edwards, although he would score some crucial goals as the season progressed.

As they had in the previous season, Leeds struggled to find any consistency, winning two and losing two of the opening four games. A rare win at Oakwell on the 2nd of September proved a bitter-sweet moment for Baird when, after scoring what proved to be the winner, he was sent off following an incident with Larry May.

The inconsistent run of results continued and despite being unbeaten in October, Leeds lost their first three games the following month. Another battering at Stoke City's Victoria Ground followed. The Potters were 5-0 up at half-time, and ran out 7-2 winners. It prompted Billy Bremner to publicly slate his players.

The Christmas and New Year results were indifferent and in a West Yorkshire derby, Huddersfield Town held Leeds to a 1-1 draw at Elland Road. The game turned out to be Ian Snodin's last for the club. With the giant vultures of English football circling, Baird had known that it would only be a matter of time before his mate would be on the move,

"Due to the fact I was travelling in with Snod, I knew what was happening. Kenny Dalglish at Liverpool along with Howard Kendall and Colin Harvey at Everton were contacting him. Today it is known as 'tapping him up'. In the end, Snod chose Everton. Billy did the negotiations and got Ian a fantastic deal at Goodison Park. The fact that Everton and Liverpool were the top two clubs in the country at that time, proves how good a player Ian Snodin was."

The Elland Road board allowed Bremner to strengthen the squad with the money received for their departing captain, and the players who arrived were experienced campaigners who were all playing their football in the top flight.

Micky Adams, who came from Coventry City, operated on the left-hand side and was comfortable at left back or in midfield. Welsh international midfielder Mark Aizlewood, who never really endeared himself to the Leeds fans, arrived from Charlton Athletic. With him came John Pearson, affectionately known as the 'Big Bird', who was a tall, lanky centre forward.

Adams and Pearson both made their debuts at home to Blackburn Rovers. Prior to the game, the striker found himself having to front Ian Baird:

"Billy told me I was wearing the number 9 shirt but that posed a problem as Bairdy was already changed and had the shirt on his back. I was terrified to ask him for it."

This was a classic case of Ian's reputation going before him. Baird willingly handed over the number 9 shirt and wore number ten. The pair got on well, they struck up a good partnership on the field and Baird appreciated the work that the Big Bird put in:

"John was a great lad, who helped me develop as a player and probably didn't get the credit he deserved. He always won his fair share of headers and his unselfish play created many goals for me. He took the knocks, although he ran like he had a grand piano on his back.

"Keith Edwards rarely got a look-in once John arrived at the club. Big things were expected of Keith when he joined during the previous summer, from Sheffield United where he had scored for fun, but he didn't get the breaks at Leeds and it wasn't happening for him."

Although losing the influential midfield presence of Ian Snodin, Leeds' season kicked into gear. John Sheridan played the leading role and Baird was scoring goals, the new lads gelled and the Whites went on a fantastic run in league and cup:

"We had a new-found confidence, and we were flying. From the turn of the year to the end of the regular season, we lost just five games in all competitions. We were attacking glory on two fronts, the FA Cup and the chase for promotion."

The FA Cup third round draw handed Leeds a tricky tie away at perennial non-league giant-killers Telford United. On the advice of Shropshire police, the game was played on a Sunday lunch-time at West Bromwich Albion's Hawthorns ground.

Gary Edwards remembers the afternoon on which two goals from Ian Baird earned Leeds a place in round four:

"The Telford game epitomised Baird's steely determination. It was a freezing cold January afternoon, the pitch was white over and dangerously rock hard. There was absolutely no way that this game should have gone ahead. But obviously anticipating an upset, the authorities allowed the game to proceed on a surface that looked more like an ice rink than a football pitch. The Leeds fans were bobbing up and down to keep warm.

"The game itself, as expected in the conditions, was a farce and could quite literally have gone either way. But Bairdy provided two superbly executed goals, one in each half, to edge Leeds through."

Baird's winning goal, scored with only five minutes to go, was tough on Telford and the striker was grateful to see the ball hit the net:

"We were on a hiding to nothing that day. We were settling for a draw in what had been a tough game in testing conditions, but thankfully I got the winning goal."

The victory set Leeds up for another banana-skin of a tie, this time against Swindon Town who were flying in Division Three. Fog prevented the tie being played on its original scheduled date and the game eventually went ahead on the following Tuesday night.

Swindon deservedly took the lead after only 12 minutes. Leeds levelled through a fortunate own goal and once again it was left to Baird, who headed Leeds in front 12 minutes into the second half. The passage to round five was sealed thanks to Mervyn Day, who made a string of fine saves to deny the plucky hosts.

For the first time in the cup run, Leeds were handed a home draw as they entered the fifth round. Londoners Queens Park Rangers, from the First Division, were the visitors and a capacity crowd packed into Elland Road, with many more locked outside.

It was Baird who gave Leeds the lead, keeping up his impressive record of scoring in every round. There were just 17 minutes gone when a cross from

Micky Adams was flicked on by Pearson and Baird, in his typically determined style, launched himself to head Leeds in front.

QPR looked like earning an undeserved draw when David Rennie put one through his own goal, but Brendan Ormsby had other ideas. Once again big John Pearson was involved, flicking on a John Sheridan corner – and the captain powered a header past David Seaman, right in front of the adoring masses situated on the Kop.

The crowd went wild. Ormsby jumped on the perimeter fencing in sheer delight. Elland Road had not witnessed such jubilant scenes since the 1970s and the fans began to sense that an unlikely trip to Wembley was in reach.

Next up was another problematic tie, this time against Wigan Athletic at Springfield Park. In the days preceding the fixture, confusion reigned as to whether or not Ian Baird would be eligible to play.

He was to serve a two-game ban, following an accumulation of yellow cards which gave him 21 disciplinary points. Leeds were scheduled to play Grimsby Town on Saturday the 7th of March, and had re-arranged a fixture against Portsmouth for the following Tuesday night.

Leeds assumed that Baird's ban would be served by missing those two games and he would be available for selection at Wigan. Incidentally, the captain, Brendan Ormsby was in the same position. The ban would give Keith Edwards the chance to impress and possibly keep Ian out of the quarter-final, and Ian had his concerns:

"I was gutted to miss two games but I was just hoping I would be back in the side for the Wigan tie. Keith was a good lad and because things had not gone to plan for him at Leeds, I wanted him to do well, but after scoring in every round I was desperate to be back in and help Leeds into the semi-final."

Baird was well aware that his physical approach was landing him in trouble on a regular basis:

"The gaffer had been encouraging me to hold back from some of the challenges I went in for, but a lot of the time it was my reputation that got me into bother. I had one of the worst disciplinary records in the league and was intent on improving it due to the amount of money it was costing me."

In the end, Ian had no need to worry about missing the cup tie due to the form of Keith Edwards. The Football Association intervened, ordering that

Baird (and Ormsby) were to serve their bans by missing the Grimsby and Wigan games. They would be free to play at Fratton Park. Effectively, rather than imposing a two-match ban on the players, they ordered them to serve two one-match bans.

The authorities believed that Leeds had purposely re-arranged the Portsmouth game to free up their leading scorer and captain for the cup tie. Leeds argued that was not the case and by re-arranging the Pompey fixture they were risking the chance of injuries meaning more players could potentially miss the quarter-final.

Unfortunately for Leeds, Baird and Ormsby, the decision stood. At Wigan, John Pearson partnered Keith Edwards up front as goals from the unlikeliest of sources – Micky Adams and John Stiles – saw the Whites win the game 2-0, setting up a semi-final tie at Hillsborough against First Division side Coventry City.

Leeds had hit a rich vein of form in the league and the visit to Portsmouth had produced a well-earned point. But the game also produced more disciplinary concerns for Ian Baird.

David Elleray was the referee that night and the official was the subject of media attention following an incident involving Leeds' fiery centre-forward.

As the players left the field for half-time, Elleray was confronted on the pitch by a policeman who alleged that Ian had made a 'V' sign to the Portsmouth fans earlier in the game:

"It transpired that Elleray was asked to come into our dressing room and warn me that I could be arrested after the game. He didn't come in there, but he spoke to me as we ran out for the second half.

"I protested my innocence. I didn't make the gesture, but the story was all over the newspapers the following morning and I was charged with bringing the game into disrepute. As a result, there was a chance I would miss the semi-final of the FA Cup."

Less than three weeks later, Ian Baird had one of his finest moments in a Leeds shirt when, on Saturday the 28th of March 1987, he scored a sensational hat-trick in a thumping 4-0 victory over Plymouth Argyle at Elland Road.

Baird, who was 'brought down' for Leeds' first goal – a John Sheridan penalty – later admitted he fell. He rightfully picked up the Man of the Match award following a dazzling display.

He side-footed home his first goal after 40 minutes, scored his second just after the hour mark following John Pearson's knock down and completed his treble with a bullet header from a Jack Ashurst cross, ensuring he walked away with the match ball for the first time in his career.

It was during the week after his heroics that Ian was cleared to play in the Hillsborough showdown. Having always claimed he was innocent, he appealed against all charges. No date had been fixed for the hearing, but he would have had 14 days to appeal any decision that may go against him. Time was on Baird's side, so thankfully he could take his place in the side as Leeds battled to overcome the final hurdle and reach Wembley.

The weekend before the Coventry game, Baird notched his 17th goal of the season in a 2-0 home win over Millwall which was followed by a goalless draw at Hull. Leeds and Ian were in a buoyant mood,

"We had a great spirit at the club and we were optimistic that we could beat the Sky Blues. But we knew that they had a good side which included the likes of big Cyrille Regis, Dave Bennett, Keith Houchen, Steve Ogrizovic, Trevor Peake and Brian Kilcline who were very good players, performing in the First Division.

"There was a massive incentive for the lads. We all wanted to play in the cup final at Wembley and we wanted to give those long-suffering supporters a day out that they would never forget.

"The Leeds supporters were unbelievable that day at Hillsborough. Everywhere we travelled they were with us, and we wanted to win so badly - not only for us but for Billy and the fans."

Football can be a cruel game and despite Leeds battling valiantly, they would lose the tie 3-2 after extra-time.

Obviously everybody connected with Leeds United was devastated at missing out on a trip to Wembley, but Billy Bremner had to lift himself and his players to focus on their one remaining target: a place in the inaugural Football League play-offs. The minimum requirement was a fifth-place finish in the final league table.

Eight games were left and after winning five of them, Leeds ended the season in fourth place. That meant a two-legged affair with Oldham Athletic, who had finished third. But Baird still had possible FA action and a suspension hanging over him:

"Unbelievably the situation following the alleged incident at Portsmouth had not been resolved, despite the fact that the Football Association had received some letters from the home fans saying I was innocent. They eventually agreed that any hearing should be held after the play-offs."

Leeds overcame Oldham after two incredibly tight games. Keith Edwards came off the bench to score in both legs as Leeds won through to a two-legged final against Charlton Athletic, who were battling to save their First Division status.

Both ties ended in 1-0 wins to the home side. Leeds would eventually lose out in a replay at Birmingham's St Andrews ground, despite taking the lead in extra time through an exquisite John Sheridan strike:

"When Shez scored his brilliant free-kick, I thought we had done it, I thought we were up. We had been comfortable during the game and I could not see how Charlton were going to turn things around.

"We were minutes away from promotion, and then Peter Shirtliff popped up with two late goals. To have our dream snatched away in that manner was awful – it was a horrible feeling, and the worst possible end to the season having felt the same way after losing to Coventry City in the FA Cup.

"I finished the 1986-87 season as Leeds United's top scorer with 19 goals. But my contract had expired and the club had not approached me about a new deal, which really disappointed me."

Just days after the season had ended in such heartbreaking fashion, Dave Blakey – Billy's chief scout – sat outside Ian's house all day, waiting to speak to him. But as far as Ian was concerned it was too little too late:

"I ignored Dave, he sat there for hours. The club should have done more to keep me, they let the situation rumble on and I thought I deserved a bit better treatment than what I got."

Ian's goal-scoring exploits at Elland Road, along with his work ethic had not gone unnoticed. Queens Park Rangers, West Ham United, Portsmouth, Celtic and Aberdeen all showed interest. The Rotherham-born hit man was very much in demand, and he was obviously looking for the best deal:

"I have to be honest, I was chasing money. I was on £300 a week at Leeds and knew I could get more. I received an offer from Portsmouth which more than doubled what I was on at Leeds, and in addition there was a car and £30,000 over three years. I travelled to Parkhead to talk to the Scottish giants Celtic; Billy McNeil offered me £500 a week to sign. He said he couldn't offer me anything more, as he had Scottish Internationals who weren't on what I wanted. I advised him it wasn't enough and told him of the offer from Pompey. 'But this is Celtic. You're coming to play for Celtic,' he told me."

In the midst of sorting out his future, Ian Baird was summoned in front of the Football Association. A hearing in Leeds focused on his disciplinary problems, among them the incident back in March at Fratton Park:

"I had totalled 41 points, but the treatment I got was scandalous. I was fined £200 and banned for the first two games of the new season. Norman Whiteside had reached the same amount of points as me, and he only received half the fine that I did. They also did me for another £100 for the Portsmouth incident."

# 10

# A Fratton Park nightmare

Dave Webb, the ex-Chelsea star, was a good friend of Ian's father. It was he who persuaded the striker not to go north of the border – advising Ian that the only place to play was the English First Division. As a result of Webb's advice, coupled with much self-contemplation, Ian decided to reject Celtic's approaches. Celtic turned their attention to West Ham United's Frank McAvennie, who signed in the October, and the Scottish giants went on to win the league and cup double.

In the meantime, Alan Ball was promising Ian the Earth at Portsmouth and he duly won the battle for the bustling centre-forward's signature. The fee would be settled by a Football League tribunal. Despite the disappointing end to an enjoyable time in West Yorkshire, Ian harboured mixed feelings:

"Although I was determined to prove myself in the top flight, I was very disappointed to leave Leeds United. I had been very happy there and the fans were magnificent to me."

He also believed that playing in the First Division would enhance his chances of winning a Scotland cap. The then national boss, Andy Roxburgh, had watched Ian playing for Leeds the previous season – and despite Ian having played for England schoolboys, he qualified to play for the Tartan Army:

"People presumed my father was Scottish and John Stiles, at Leeds, would sometimes refer to me as 'Jocky McBaird'.

"I'd had a chat with Billy Bremner towards the end of the 1986-87 season, and he had informed me that Scotland were ready to select me for an international friendly during the summer."

However, things didn't work out on the international scene. When the Scottish FA looked into Pat Baird's background, they soon realised he had been born in the Republic of Ireland:

"The squad was about to be announced, and the Scottish FA didn't have time to delve into the family history, I would have qualified to represent the Scots through my fathers roots but it just wasn't to be."

Ian often refers to the 'Baird bad luck', and the situation with Scotland is one example where it is evident.

Having played for Portsmouth's bitter rivals, Southampton, Ian understood that he had a battle on his hands to win over the Pompey faithful .They were obviously aware of his roots and had always given him plenty of stick in the past.

As he plotted his assault on England's top flight, Alan Ball had also brought in another ex-Leeds United striker: Terry Connor, from Brighton and Hove Albion. His main man the previous seasons had been Micky Quinn, who he tried to offload . Ironically there was reported interest from Leeds.

Quinn had a well-earned reputation for being an excellent finisher. His goalscoring record was second to none, and Ian remembers that even after Micky had scored in training he used to wheel away in celebration:

"He wasn't the fittest player in the country and he wasn't the most technically gifted but he was a natural goalscorer, and after bagging 28 goals in Pompey's promotion season he quite rightly deserved a crack at the First Division. Even in training he was desperate to score and when he did he would celebrate.

"Micky was a top lad who was good for morale and was always cracking jokes. He dug his heels in and didn't leave."

On the day that Ian reported for his first day of pre-season training, he knew he had a fight on his hands to secure a first team place – particularly with the two-match suspension hanging over him. In addition to Connor and Quinn, there was Paul Mariner, the ex-Ipswich Town and England international, to provide further competition. But from the moment he walked into the club, Baird never got a feel for the place:

"Micky Fillery and Ian Stewart had also joined Pompey that summer, and we all felt there was very much a 'them and us' situation with the old guard. Also, the cheque I received for the signing-on fee had bounced, and almost instantly

I knew I had made a massive mistake. Once again I had totally fucked up, and it is one of the biggest regrets of my career not going to Parkhead."

Right from the start nothing went to plan, and the preparation for the new campaign did nothing to lift Ian's spirits:

"We went to an Army camp and ran our bollocks off before a pre-season tour to Sweden. Where we stayed was such a depressing place. There was nothing to do and I could understand why it was dubbed the suicide capital of Europe. Things went wrong from the start; Connor, Vince Hilaire and big Noel Blake were too busy in the duty free store at Heathrow and missed the plane. Bally was beside himself, he was quite rightly going mental.

"The time we spent over there in Sweden, we trained, played a few friendlies and got pissed. There was a serious drinking culture within the club, which for a newly promoted side wasn't the ideal preparation for the season ahead."

It was a familiar start for Ian on the tour. He scored three times in four games but was also booked in three of those matches. Proof that even in friendly games, the bustling striker did not hold back in his desire to win the game.

Whilst in Sweden, Ian spoke to the media about a death threat that he had received following the move to Fratton Park:

"I received a letter which told me if I went into Southampton at night on my own, I'd be done in. I'm not going to worry about that sort of thing. It's not very nice but I'm going to get on with playing games. I know I've got a job on to win over the Fratton Park fans and there would be no better way to do it than score a couple against Saints."

The Football League tribunal to determine the fee that Leeds would receive for Ian's services took place following Portsmouth's return from Scandinavia. Leeds had valued Ian at £500,000, whilst Portsmouth's valuation was significantly lower at £100,000.

Portsmouth were threatening to pull the plug on the deal if they were ordered to pay a fee they deemed unfair. However, at the tribunal held in London, Ian's new employers were ordered to pay £285,000 and subsequently the deal went through.

The season got underway, and Portsmouth lost the opening two games without their suspended striker:

"I served my suspension and came straight into the side for my debut against Southampton on the 22nd of August, in a 2-2 draw. A right hammering at Arsenal followed but then we started to pick up a few points, going five league games unbeaten.

"We played Charlton Athletic at home and there had been a bit of history between myself and Paul Miller. Miller said something to me during the game and it resulted in me losing my cool. I turned around and landed a punch on him for which the referee gave me a red card, which resulted in a three game ban.

"As I walked off, Miller shouted over, 'See you later son, you've been suckered again.'"

Vince Hilaire, one of Ian's team-mates that day, spoke of the incident:

"I used to drive into training with Bairdy as we lived close to one another. On the way to the ground that morning he was in good spirits. He was yet to score for Portsmouth, but felt he was finding his feet and was starting to make a contribution. He was telling me that he had grown up a little bit and was capable of imposing some self control.

"I knew 'Maxi' Miller and he could dish it out verbally, he was the master at winding people up. He said something to Ian who completely lost it.

"The incident did Bairdy no favours whatsoever, and the gaffer was far from happy. The last thing he did before we crossed the white line was to remind Ian not to let Miller wind him up."

Ian sat through yet another suspension and, although he got straight back into the side, the rot had already set in:

"I couldn't gel with the lads, I wasn't enjoying training and I couldn't score a goal. I managed just one in my Portsmouth career. It came at Loftus Road in a 2-1 defeat to Queens Park Rangers, in what was my ninth start for the club."

The goal, was well overdue, and at Portsmouth's next home game – against Sheffield Wednesday – the street vendors were selling tee-shirts which claimed, 'I was there when Bairdy scored'.

Alan Knight, Portsmouth's goalkeeper and iconic figure at Fratton Park, recognised Baird's frustrations:

"Ian was a great lad, but it never happened for him at Portsmouth and with him being ex-Southampton he was up against it from the start. He worked hard but the goals didn't come. Eventually he realised he was fighting a losing battle, particularly with the fans.

"I walked into the changing rooms one day after training, and Bairdy was sat there with his head in his hands. I asked him if everything was OK. He looked up at me and moaned, 'What a fucking shit-hole this place is.'"

Ian went from one nightmare to another, and decided to go in and have a one-to-one with his manager Alan Ball, a guy he looked up to. Ball told Ian to keep plugging away, and acknowledged that the wingers were not getting the balls into the box like they had done the previous season. Kevin O'Callaghan had left to join Millwall and Portsmouth were missing his creative wing play:

"I was pleased with that. I thought I'd got the support of the gaffer, and that meant a lot to me. I gained some confidence from that. We then played Everton at home, a top team full of fantastic players. Despite having Mick Kennedy and Kevin Dillon sent off we worked our socks off, only to lose to a late goal from Graeme Sharp, and Bally seemed relatively pleased with the performance.

"We had the Monday off and on the Tuesday Bally called a team meeting. I was sat next to Vince Hilaire; the boss was raging and told a few people a few home truths. Eventually, it was my turn and he really ripped into me.

"'You come to me telling me you are struggling and you can't score. I'll tell you why you can't score – you can't even score in training, never mind on a Saturday!'"

From that moment, Ian lost all respect for a man he had thought so much of. A man he had confided in, only to be hammered in front of the whole squad.

"I realised from that point that Pompey were trying to sell me. I started getting phone calls from other clubs. Barnsley and Hull City were interested, but I was never going to consider either of those two. Ball told me it was a situation he had no control over, as it had become apparent that the Chairman had no money. I couldn't believe the situation I had found myself in. Portsmouth had hung me out to dry."

Ian felt vulnerable, to the point that he did not want to play on a Saturday. The Pompey fans were on his back, he was the club-record signing who wasn't putting the ball into the net. He was ex-Southampton, Portsmouth were struggling, and he had become the obvious target for the boo boys.

Things came to a head when Ball was eventually told he had to sell Ian and Mick Kennedy. There was a lot of interest in both players, and Kennedy joined Bradford City for £250,000 in January 1988. The view of many a Pompey fan is that the day Kennedy left was the day Portsmouth Football Club accepted they would be relegated back to the Second Division come May.

# 11

# Returning 'home'

Ian had no choice but to hang around a little longer at Portsmouth and bide his time, but eventually he would get the move he desperately craved:

"Whilst at Portsmouth I had stayed in touch with a few of the lads back at Leeds, and also the physiotherapist, Alan Sutton – who knew that I wanted to return to West Yorkshire despite interest from the other clubs.

"Sutty had informed me that there had been pressure on Billy following a poor start to the season, when Leeds really struggled to score goals. They had signed Jim Melrose but he never managed a goal for the club and would soon be on his way out.

"At that time, I would have re-signed for Billy under any circumstances. I travelled up to Elland Road and met Dave Blakey, who advised me that the offer was the same wages as I had been on at Fratton Park and I would receive a signing-on fee. It was a case of take it or leave it.

"I instantly accepted it, and without a second's hesitation I signed the forms which ensured I got the move I had hankered for. My nightmare spell at Portsmouth was over and I was a very happy man."

However, there was one more battle to be won, with the Pompey Chairman. It was a battle over the ownership of a motor vehicle:

"When I joined Portsmouth, there was a brand new Toyota Corolla Sport included in the signing-on package. Deacon, the Chairman, was a very successful local businessman who didn't like parting with money – and as the move back to Elland Road was going through, he knew that the club had made a loss on the transfer fee and he was in damage limitation mode.

"He tried to screw me over and take back the vehicle. I wasn't having any of it, and told him that I'd sold the car to an independent motor dealer who traded under the name of Philip James Motors."

Philip James Motors was a figment of Ian's imagination. Philip and James are the middle names of Jerry Hilton and Ian. Deacon contacted 'Phillip James Motors' but unbeknown to him, he was speaking to Jerry:

"Deacon contacted me and tried to claim the car; I advised him that I'd purchased it from Ian Baird in good faith. Therefore, I needed Deacon to pay off the finance, which would enable me to have 'clean title' to go on and sell the motor to regain my supposed capital.

"He put up a bit of a fight and I'm sure he suspected we were in cahoots, but he was unable to prove anything. Needless to say, he cleared the finance and a much sought-after Toyota Corolla was sold on to a local dealer, meaning Ian came out of it with the money."

Having seen the experience of being at Portsmouth affect Ian in the way that it did, Vince Hilaire knew what the move meant to him:

"Words can't capture how happy Bairdy was when the move finally went through. He was desperate to return to Elland Road, and when he said his goodbyes to me I could see that the weight of the world had been lifted from his shoulders. He was absolutely over the moon, although he's never let me forget that I only created one goal for him at Fratton Park. Little did we know that I would be following him up there a few months later."

Ian acknowledges that although the spell at Portsmouth was an absolute nightmare, he left there a better player after working with Alan Ball. However, the whole experience left a bitter taste in his mouth and in an interview with a popular weekly football magazine; he admitted that he never wanted to see Fratton Park or John Deacon again.

There is no doubt that Baird's return to Leeds gave the club and the fans a massive boost in what had been an indifferent season. Midfield dynamo John Sheridan was quick to welcome Ian back to Elland Road, and he knew it would benefit the side:

"It was a big boost for us. There wasn't a defender in the league who liked playing against Ian. They knew they would be in for a tough afternoon with his uncompromising style."

Baird admitted that the Leeds fans would not see much change in his approach; aggression was still very much part of his game. And one man who was soon on the receiving end was manager Billy Bremner when, in the first training session following Ian's return, he and Baird clashed:

"Billy would run onto the muddy, waterlogged pitches of Fullerton Park wearing Adidas Sambas when all the lads had studs, yet he was still the best player at Leeds.

"During my first training session, I nailed him in a challenge, and at first it was feared his leg was broken. But he was fine and he said very little about the incident. I thought I'd got away with it, until the following morning when he came trotting across the car park, up the concrete steps and onto the training ground. You could hear the tapping of the studs and Billy was shouting, 'These are for you Bairdy'."

Glynn Snodin acknowledged that the training ground could be a tough, competitive place – even on a Friday:

"Training on a Friday could be mayhem, we had some great times. You would think that we'd have taken it easy with a game coming the following day, but the gaffer used to bring a box of Milk Tray chocolates in for the winners of the 5-a-side. Everybody went hell for leather. It was great when we got back into the dressing room, we would tease the lads who had been on the losing side with the chocolates. Bairdy loved those games and he never held back, particularly when Norman Hunter, who was coach then, got himself involved. They would kick lumps out of each other."

Ironically, Ian's second debut – at home to Plymouth Argyle on the 5th of March 1988 – marked the occasion of his 100th appearance in a Leeds shirt. And despite receiving a booking following a challenge on Argyle's Leigh Cooper, there was no better way to mark the occasion than by scoring the only goal of the game. He raced clear to score the crucial match-winner, which kept alive Leeds' faint hopes of finishing in a play-off place.

In his match day programme notes for the Plymouth game, Billy Bremner acknowledged how delighted he was to have brought the striker back to the club:

*'We welcome Ian Baird back to Elland Road and wish him every success as he starts his second spell with us. I don't think there was any secret that I was sorry*

*to see Ian leave us for Portsmouth last summer due to freedom of contract and I am delighted that he is back at Leeds.*

*'As you will all know, Ian is a very competitive player and has just the kind of approach we need as we enter the run in to the end of the season.'*

One Leeds fan in the ground that day was Gavin Baird, who will never forget the occasion that his older brother made his return to Elland Road:

"I was only a boy but all I could hear was a constant chant of, 'Bairdy is back!' For me, standing in the greatest football ground in the world listening to the crowd chanting that, life couldn't get any better."

Those faint play-off hopes were dashed by the start of April. After a fantastic victory at Villa Park and a thumping win over Sheffield United – in which John Pearson scored a hat-trick – Leeds claimed just one point from the next nine available with a draw at Bournemouth and successive defeats to Shrewsbury Town and Millwall.

Baird admitted after the Millwall defeat that they needed a miracle, but as far as he was concerned their chance had gone after they failed to win against Bournemouth and Shrewsbury.

Leeds didn't have a fixture on the weekend preceding the Millwall game, and the players travelled down to a hotel in Bournemouth where they would spend the weekend playing golf. Billy Bremner didn't travel with the party, and Dave Bentley was left in charge for a trip that Baird admits didn't exactly go to plan:

"We travelled down there for the weekend and on the Saturday we went to The Dell, and watched Southampton beat Arsenal 4-2 in a game which saw a young Alan Shearer score a hat-trick on his full league debut.

"For the remainder of the time, we played golf and got on the piss. We really got stuck into the booze and Bentley lost all control of the situation.

"Something really kicked off – and by the time we had returned to Leeds, the hotel had reported us all to Billy Bremner who was absolutely furious. Billy really laid into us. However, I can't tell you what happened because believe it or not, for once I wasn't involved."

Ian had found the net just once in eight games following his return to the club, but he was soon back on the goal trail:

"I played in the reserves against Grimsby Town and scored a hat-trick in a 9-2 win, which gave me some renewed confidence to take into an away game at Swindon Town where I scored twice. The season was effectively over, but it was important to finish as high in the league as possible."

Towards the end of the season there was a memorable occasion that Ian and his team-mates will never forget. It came on the evening of the 12th of April 1988, when Elland Road staged a testimonial game for Bobby Collins and John Charles. The match was played before 13,671 fans and televised live in Turin, Italy.

"It was a fantastic night. One of Bobby Collins' former clubs, Everton, provided the opposition and John Charles' former club, Juventus, allowed two of their world class players to make guest appearances. Ian Rush and Gaetano Scirea, who was unfortunately killed soon after in a car accident in Poland, came over along with the Frenchman Michel Platini who had recently retired.

"Before the kick-off, Platini was sitting in the dressing room, smoking these very expensive cigarettes and drinking plenty of coffee."

Liverpool manager Kenny Dalglish also turned out in Leeds colours, on a night when Baird was substitute and would come on to replace Ian Rush who had scored a first half hat-trick:

"When I entered the field of play I was up front with Dalglish, who was superb. He was talking to me throughout, encouraging me to work harder and close people down. Kenny played the game like it was a cup final, and I realised that night what a great bloke he was and why he had been so successful in the game."

Leeds, and guests, beat Everton 3-2. Afterwards everybody congregated in the players' lounge, where The Gentle Giant made a speech to thank everybody involved:

"Obviously he thanked the lads who had travelled over from Italy, and in doing so he said it was nice to see some quality footballers perform on Elland Road. The Leeds lads looked on in amazement. We couldn't believe it."

At the end of the season, which had seen Ian witness many ups and downs, he was once again the subject of transfer speculation – with further interest from north of the border:

"Hearts made a bid for me but it was swiftly turned down by the Chairman Leslie Silver, and although Billy also didn't want me to go, it was his duty to inform me that the bid had been made. But I wasn't interested in going there, and that was the end of the matter.

"I was enjoying my football again and we had a great set of lads in the dressing room. A young David Batty had emerged from the youth team, he was a great lad who despite his scruffy appearance displayed a tremendous amount of ability and he was as hard as nails.

"We were in a bar in Leeds one Saturday night after a home game. There was Batts, Gary Speed, my mate Jerry and one or two of the other lads. We were enjoying the banter and a few beers when were spotted by a group of females who made their way over to us.

"Jerry was chatting away to one of them when Batts decided to tell the girl that Jerry was a Spurs player who was currently out injured. They really fell for it, which was quite unbelievable. He was an overweight motor trader who smoked 20 fags a day, and there he was signing autographs.

"As we prepared for the 1988-89 season, all appeared to be rosy at the club and we were geared up for mounting a serious promotion challenge. Billy had signed two of my former colleagues from Portsmouth, Noel Blake and Vince Hilaire, and we had a good dressing room.

"After drawing 1-1 at home to Oxford United in the opening game, we had a bad run of results. And unfortunately I pressed the self-destruct button just a week into the season, when we visited Fratton Park."

It was the first time that Ian had returned to Portsmouth following his unhappy time there – and with Blake and Hilaire also playing against their former club, it all added a bit of spice to the fixture which was played on a baking hot day.

Alan Ball was aware of the threat that Bairdy posed, and he penned a warning in his match-day programme notes:

'No doubt Ian Baird will have a point or two to prove, he didn't have the happiest of times in his brief spell here last season but if I know anything about the lad, he will be out to prove that we never really saw the real Ian Baird.'

Leeds lost the game 4-0, and it would have been worse had the normally reliable Micky Quinn scored from the penalty spot. However, Baird's return to Fratton Park ended early when he was shown the red card by referee Ian Hemley:

"Quite frankly I lost control. I wasn't playing well, I was getting stick from the home crowd, I was frustrated and got myself sent off for two bookable offences.

"The Portsmouth players were appealing to the referee not to send me off but he did, and that was my afternoon finished with another suspension to serve and another fine to pay."

Throughout the two spells Ian Baird had at Leeds United, it is very difficult to find any sort of criticism which was aimed his way from people who in one way or another had an association with the club.

However, in the aftermath of the hammering at Fratton Park and Ian's red card, journalist John Wray penned a damning assessment in an article for his column in the *Bradford Telegraph & Argus*, under the headline, 'WHEN WILL BAIRD GET THE MESSAGE':

*'Manager Billy Bremner subjected wayward Leeds United striker Ian Baird to "the appropriate club discipline" for his totally unnecessary sending off at Portsmouth. Doubtless a heavy fine was imposed but Baird should be mightily relieved he didn't receive his cards.*

*'Bearing in mind his past record of dismissals and bookings it is high time the 24 year old learned to keep his aggression under control or looked for a new career in the wrestling ring.*

*'Bremner was furious with the player because he warned Baird to keep out of trouble before running out to face his old Portsmouth team mates, yet Baird apparently ignored his manager's instructions and referee Ian Hemley's warning during the game.*

*'It's bad enough to be sent off for two blatant bookable offences in any game, but to earn the red card when your team mates are desperately struggling to recover from a four goal deficit is all the more shameful.*

*'Off the field, I found Baird polite, helpful and genuinely concerned about his reputation for over stepping the disciplinary mark with referees. But with 43 bookings, nine suspensions and four sendings off over the last four years isn't it about time he did something about it before he's drummed out of the game?*

*'Incidentally Baird was booked on his debut for United at Portsmouth in March 1985 and fined £100 for making an obscene gesture to the Portsmouth crowd on another visit in March 1987. Don't ask him if Fratton Park is his lucky ground.'*

The article didn't go down too well with Ian at the time and, having served yet another suspension, he was intent on cleaning up his act.

As the club suffered a poor start to the season, Ian had to wait until the 27th of September before he found the net. It came in the first leg of a League Cup tie at Peterborough United, which would prove to be Billy Bremner's last game in charge of Leeds:

"I remember the goal, we were already 1-0 up and Batts found me with a defence-splitting pass which I put away from 12 yards."

Despite winning the game, Billy Bremner was relieved of his duties by the Elland Road board. Two members of his backroom staff, Dave Bentley and Dave Blakey, were also shown the door:

"The feeling amongst the players was very similar to the one when Eddie Gray had been sacked. I can always remember the coach journey to Peterborough and Glynn Snodin was reading a newspaper article in which it claimed that Billy was under pressure. Although results had not been great, the players didn't really believe that he was heading for the exit.

"It was a real honour to play for Billy Bremner and work with him on a daily basis. I can't speak highly enough of the man."

# 12

## A club transformed

Following Billy's dismissal, the board put their trust in Peter Gunby and Norman Hunter to take charge of first team affairs until a new appointment was made. However, Leeds' results far from improved:

"Norman had informed us that he wanted the job. Unfortunately we lost the next three games, and personally I was really struggling to find any sort of form. I had managed to score in a 2-1 defeat away at Brighton but my frustrations were increasing."

Another 2-1 defeat followed, this time against Sunderland at Roker Park, and any hopes that Hunter had of landing his dream job were fading fast. Ian was replaced in the second half and those frustrations got the better of him:

"I knew I wasn't playing well and Norman brought the Big Bird on to replace me. I came off the pitch and Norman went to shake my hand. I told him to fuck off and went straight down the tunnel. He came after me and we had a standing argument, but I soon came to my senses and apologised.

"I was bang out of order. I had no right to talk to somebody like Norman Hunter in that manner. He was a great bloke, he'd been a world class player, and I very much regretted the incident.

"It was a very frustrating time and I couldn't figure out the reasons for my poor performances and incidents like the one with Norman. I was happy at home, my daughter Amy had been born, and things were perfect away from the football."

Another incident in that evening game in Sunderland has remained in Bairdy's memory:

"Sunderland had big Billy Whitehurst up front. Whitehurst was a hard man who took no prisoners, and as soon as Sunderland had kicked off they hammered the ball over to the left-hand side where Billy was. He came straight across our left back, Micky Adams, and completely wiped him out. Micky was laid out at the side of the pitch not having a clue what had happened to him. The game wasn't even a minute old."

By the time Leeds travelled to Swindon Town on the 16th of October, the board had got their man. Howard Wilkinson was appointed as Billy's replacement, in a move that would transform the club's fortunes:

"Wilkinson entered Elland Road like a whirlwind and instantly began to stamp his authority on the place. It is well documented that he removed the pictures of the glory days from the walls and, rightly or wrongly, that was just the start.

"Training was very different. Under Billy we would train from ten o'clock until eleven-thirty, then we'd have a bite to eat and go home. Under Wilkinson we were there until four o'clock in the afternoon, working our way through two sessions a day, and it was like that for four months.

"He was renowned for his training methods and the running his players would do, and all we did to start with was run our bollocks off. It helped us psychologically, it certainly made us more aware and it definitely made us fitter.

"Wilkinson opened up our minds as to how times were changing. It was the little things; we started drinking Gatorade rather than blackcurrant with lemonade or cups of tea, and we were given vitamin tablets to take. He educated us as footballers, he made me a better player and for that I have total respect for him as a football manager. Although he's not the most popular man in the world and he certainly wouldn't be on my Christmas card list.

"He was a shouter and a screamer, but he made you want to play for him. He was also very boring and regimental, he played mind games with us and he displayed an extremely strange sense of humour. On many occasions, he called Bobby Davison 'Dave'. After a while Bobby got fed up with it and told Wilkinson that his name was in fact Bobby. Wilko barked at him, 'When you start playing well, I'll call you Bobby'.

"He was very close to Bill Fotherby, and you knew he would rejuvenate the club and be given the money to get the right players for the job in hand. I focused on knuckling down, working hard, playing well and staying in the team.

"His assistant, Mick Hennigan was a completely different character. Very thorough and professional, but he was an all-round nice bloke with a burning desire to succeed. He was a good man to have around the place and he really bonded with the lads."

In Wilkinson's first game in charge, Leeds halted a run of four successive league defeats with a 0-0 draw at Swindon, and results dramatically improved. Baird and Bobby Davison were forming a deadly partnership, and it wasn't until the 10th of December that Wilkinson suffered his first league defeat – in a surprise 3-2 reverse at home to Shrewsbury Town.

Mike Whitlow was signed from non-league side Witton Albion early in Wilkinson's reign at Leeds, and he remembers Baird's 'enthusiasm' on Fullerton Park during his first training session:

"I never really had much to do with Ian at Leeds if I am being honest. I was in awe of the place, and used to sit in the corner on my own and then disappear after training. By the time I had started to join in with the banter, Ian had moved on.

"I joined Leeds with Neil Parsley, and in our first training session Baird welcomed Neil to the club by cutting him in half with a ferocious challenge. It was a greeting that Neil hadn't expected."

Baird and Sheridan were regulars at events held by the Kippax Branch of the Leeds United Supporters Club. In December 1988, they attended an event held at *Upstairs Downstairs*, a bar in Armley, along with David Batty and Bobby Davison. Gary Edwards, the author of '*Paint it White*', remembers the occasion:

"On that particular night the draw for the third round of the FA Cup was being made, and the partying was temporarily brought to a stop as people focused on the various televisions within the establishment to watch the draw.

"Leeds were presented with a trip to the Goldstone Ground to play Brighton & Hove Albion and the moment our ball came out of the bag, Bairdy and Shez leapt onto the tables. Shez grabbed a microphone and started singing 'Marching on Together', which was followed by a chorus of 'Wem-ber-ley, Wem-ber-ley' to which everyone joined in. There was beer everywhere, and Shez fell off a table and broke the microphone."

It was in that FA Cup tie that Baird produced one of his finest performances of the season, when his two goals saw Leeds overcome Albion and progress to the fourth round with a 2-1 win.

Leeds had rapidly climbed the table under Wilkinson's stewardship. But three games without a win at the start of March halted their progress and Sergeant Wilko, as he had become affectionately known, began to make the changes he felt were desperately needed.

On transfer deadline day in March 1989, Leeds United sent out a real statement of intent to the rest of the sides in the Second Division. Howard Wilkinson brought in the flame-haired Scot Gordon Strachan, who had been written off by many people.

Strachan was joined by stylish central defender Chris Fairclough who arrived from Tottenham Hotspur, and striker Carl Shutt who joined from Bristol City in a part exchange for Bob Taylor.

Baird was impressed by Strachan and the methods and ideas he brought to Elland Road,

"Strach was on another level to the rest of us. He would eat bananas, porridge and take seaweed tablets – the rest of us had never seen anything like it. We had a canteen at the ground and the ladies that worked in there were brilliant but, to be honest, the food was shit.

"On a Friday we would be given fish, chips and mushy peas, which was a million miles away from Gordon's diet and the way he fuelled his body ahead of the weekend game.

"Every aspect of the way we were looked after was totally different in my time. We never had the sports scientists and the technology that's available today and it took us longer to get over injuries. If you weren't sure that you were fit to play, the medical staff would give you a jab and you were sent out onto the field.

"I once had a pain in the sole of my foot and Alan Sutton informed me that a jab would sort it out. He pulled out this huge needle and told me it wouldn't hurt. The needle went in and the pain was unbearable, although it enabled me to get my boots on and play 90 minutes. I was unaware that, as a result of all the injections, I would suffer like I do today.

"I suffer terribly, especially in my ankles, and I am constantly taking prescribed anti-inflammatory tablets to ease the chronic aches and pains."

The 1988-89 campaign would ultimately prove to be Ian's last full season as a Leeds United player – and it was marked by him winning a fantastic accolade when he was voted the Leeds United Supporters Club Player of the Year.

Although extremely proud to have won the award, it came as a big surprise to the hard-working front man, especially after a very difficult start to the season:

"It was the first award I had ever won in professional football. The supporters are at the forefront of the club and I always had a superb relationship with the Leeds fans. It was a great honour and very satisfying."

Leeds finished the season in 10ᵗʰ place and faced at least another year in the Second Division. But under Wilkinson, the club was set for take-off.

The summer of 1989 was like no other that Leeds United fans had ever experienced. Having stabilised the team since his arrival at the club, Wilkinson shuffled his pack with devastating effect.

The transfer system worked differently in those days and players could come and go during the season, at any time up to the last Thursday in March. Loan moves were not as common as they are today – but looking at the way Wilkinson did his business that summer, you would have thought a transfer window had been enforced.

The signings were dubbed the 'Magnificent Seven' by the media. Mel Sterland arrived from Scottish giants Glasgow Rangers. John Hendrie, the subject of Leeds interest under Billy Bremner, finally moved to Elland Road from Newcastle United. The experienced trio of John McClelland, Jim Beglin and Mickey Thomas joined Wilkinson's revolution as did Chris O'Donnell, a youngster from Ipswich Town.

There was one more signing, and it had the journalists sharpening their pencils and the majority of people scratching their heads – wondering why Wilkinson had spent £650,000 on a midfielder from Wimbledon who was seemingly attached to controversy with a magnet:

"Vinnie was a great lad, although I feel he exaggerated matters in his book about the divide at club. There was a divide, but that is only natural with so many new signings and a few players who knew they had no future and that their days were numbered. I had experienced the same when I joined Portsmouth and it happens all the time.

"He was a larger than life character, and I think it's fair to say that Vinnie really improved as a player during his time at Leeds."

A lot has been said and written about Vinnie Jones, and he arrived at Leeds intent on making sure nobody treated him like an idiot. He took no liberties and there was the incident in the players' lounge involving Bobby Davison, which was soon forgotten as the club embarked on its mission to return to the top flight.

Leeds supporters everywhere could not wait for the season to get underway. Once again the bookmakers installed Leeds as promotion favourites, and everybody believed that the long-awaited return to the First Division was only nine months away:

"We started the season at Newcastle, who had been relegated the previous season. At half-time we deservedly went in 2-1 up but nobody could have envisaged what would happen in the second half. For some reason I ended up playing in midfield, and Micky Quinn tore us apart. We were missing some key players that day but the 5-2 defeat really hurt, and we knew we had to get something in the following fixture against Middlesbrough on the Wednesday night so that we were up and running."

Leeds coughed and spluttered their way through the opening fixtures but a solitary goal scored by Ian Baird at Hull City on the 16th of September gave Leeds three points and finally plans clicked into place:

"We had some sticky performances, but nobody panicked despite the fact that there was a mountain of pressure on us. We drew a lot of games early on but we knew that sooner or later we would give some team a good hiding, which we did when we destroyed Swindon 4-0. And from then on we were unstoppable."

Leeds were soon right in the thick of things at the top of the league. But Bairdy was struggling to find the net although he was creating goals for Bobby Davison, who appreciated what his strike partner was all about:

"Bairdy would do his homework on the opposition and I remember one time before we played Blackburn. They came to Elland Road early on in our promotion season. Somebody had wound Bairdy up, telling him that Colin Hendry's father had been on the phone to Wilko telling him that his son wanted to play for Leeds.

"For the whole game Bairdy was at Hendry, constantly telling him that he'd never play for Leeds because he wasn't good enough. He dished out some real stick and he loved that type of situation.

"I played alongside some quality centre-forwards throughout my career, and Ian was a very, very good footballer. Everybody at Leeds appreciated what Ian brought to the side, and he had a lot more to his game that just being a bustling centre-forward.

"He was good in the air, he was superb at holding the ball up and he knew where the net was, although admittedly he did have a nasty streak.

"In one game, I had scored from a tight angle and I ran to celebrate in front of the Kop. The opposition's goalkeeper was laid on the ground and Bairdy stood on him as he ran across to celebrate with me. None of the officials saw it, and the incident passed by without any punishment being dished out.

"We had a visual analysis room at Elland Road, where we would watch videos of previous matches. And as we were watching the re-run of that game, Wilko saw the incident, rewound the tape and made us watch it again. He never said a word to Bairdy, but it was his way of letting him know he was aware of what happened and he was far from impressed."

Despite that, Baird's disciplinary record was much improved and he admitted that he was a changed character following a stark warning from his manager:

"Wilkinson told me in no uncertain terms that if I did not buckle down and change my ways then I would not be playing. I had got a reputation that pre-ceded me and referees would pick up on that. I had never been one for dissent and answering back, but some of my tackles were reckless and that was the problem. I made a conscious effort to change and I was starting to grow up and calm down. The proof was there, I got booked against Sunderland in a highly charged affair, and that was my first for about 20 games."

Gordon Strachan was pivotal to everything that Leeds United achieved in the 1989-90 season, and as the club captain he saw and appreciated the change in Baird's ways:

"When I first joined Leeds United, I got the impression that everybody liked to flex their muscles and play the hard guy. That had to change and it did. Ian Baird was a very good footballer who adapted his game quite quickly under Howard Wilkinson.

"Ian was skilful for a big man, and he was excellent in the air. He feared nobody on the opposition, but a player is of no benefit to anyone when he's sat in the stands serving suspensions on a regular basis, and once he cut out the silly challenges and needless bookings, he became a far better player."

When Leeds entertained Bournemouth at the start of November, Baird ended a run of nine league games without a goal when he headed Leeds in front. 'The slumbering giant had awoken', said John Helm, who was commentating on the game. Baird afterwards admitted to being relieved that the goal drought was over:

"When a lean spell without a goal is brought to the attention of the public you feel under a bit of pressure It was nice to break the sequence and the lads were happy to see me hit the target."

Ian and his first wife Lesley.

Ian and his father, Pat.

Ian, Amy and Lesley.

In the pool with Liam and Amy.

Amy following in her Grandma's footsteps.

Amy in recent times.

Tying the knot with Christina.

Family time with Christina and Neo.

Ian with brothers Darren, Gavin and father Pat.

Ian and his brothers with mum, Hilary.

Ian and Liam at Elland Road in 2013.

At the World Cup in 2002 with Hayden Evans and Peter Jackson.

A heavy night!

The programme for Ian's debut for the England schoolboys. (With kind permission of the Welsh SFA)

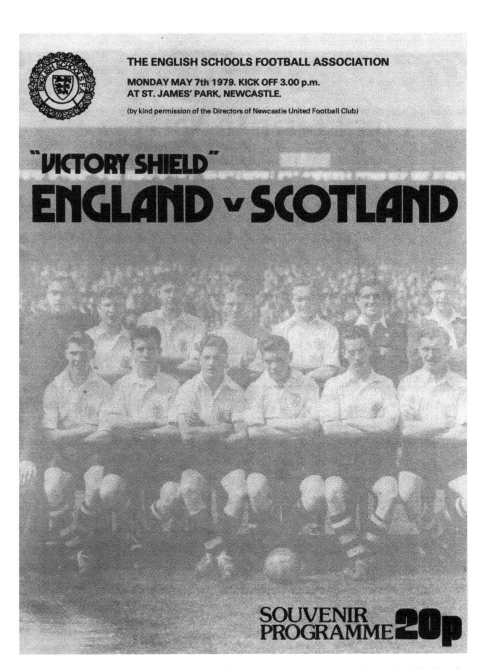

The programme from his 2nd and final cap against Scotland. (With kind permission of the English SFA)

Ian with Jerry Hilton, the pair were inseparable in their
younger days.

Early days at Southampton.

Ian celebrating one of his 58 Leeds goals.

On the cover of a Boro programme in 1991. (Courtesy of Shaun Wilson)

Re-united with Joe at Hearts.

Brighton secured their football league status with 4 points from these 2 games in 1997. (Courtesy of Mark Davey)

Coaching in Hong Kong with Khoo Luam Khen.

Ian showing he's never lost any of his 'determination' in the Hong Kong Sevens. (Courtesy of Dennis Bundy)

# 13

# Out of a promotion battle into a relegation scrap

A week after defeating Newcastle at Elland Road, Leeds travelled to Middlesbrough and due to injury, Ian would miss his first game of the season. After a substitute appearance against Brighton & Hove Albion, he was soon back in the starting line-up, but he failed to find the net in the next five games – which included a 1-0 defeat at home to Ipswich Town in the FA Cup third round:

"My form had been good and although the lack of goals was a talking point, the highest compliment I received was that Wilkinson continued to play me every week, unless I was injured. But then one evening I was relaxing at home watching Calendar news, and it was reported that Leeds had signed Lee Chapman from Nottingham Forest.

"I immediately thought, 'I'm not having that'. I was furious, and the next morning I made a point of speaking to Wilkinson who was taken aback by my approach.

"I was named as substitute for the game at Blackburn Rovers, in which Chapman made his debut and was credited with a goal that wasn't his. Blackburn missed a late penalty and I was obviously chuffed to bits that the lads had won.

"On the way home, we stopped at a hotel where we had a few beers. The lads enjoyed themselves, but I was still fuming that I had been left out.

"After playing in a Zenith Data Systems Cup tie at Villa Park, I was in training preparing for a home game against Stoke City, knowing I would be back on the bench. My body language was enough to suggest that I had well and truly spat the dummy out. Wilkinson called me in for a chat, and he explained that he wanted to me to stay and fight for my place. I told him I wasn't playing second fiddle and I wanted to go.

"Mick Hennigan told me to go home, I wasn't in the right frame of mind – and that evening, Bruce Rioch and Colin Todd came to my house to get an understanding of my situation. They were in the area as Middlesbrough were playing our promotion rivals Sheffield United at Brammall Lane the following day, and Rioch informed me that he wanted me at Ayresome Park."

Ian had made it clear that he wanted to move on but with the benefit of hindsight, leaving Leeds United at a time when the club was on the verge of returning to the big time is the biggest regret of his football career:

"Looking back I was bloody-minded. It was typical me, acting before I'd really thought about it. Lee Chapman was a proven goalscorer and his record at Leeds speaks for itself. However, just after I left Carl Shutt and Bobby Davison suffered with injuries and Leeds had to bring in Imre Varadi.

"I threw away the chance of a First Division medal and playing in Europe. Look at Shutty, he was out of the picture for a while and was even sent out on loan. But he bided his time and went on to score the winning goal in a European Cup game in the Nou Camp."

The move to the North East was the first time that Ian had used an agent when negotiating a deal, and Hayden Evans was the man he had put his trust in. Hayden had been advising Ian for a couple of years and he will never forget those eventful negotiations at Middlesbrough:

"As often happens, we were waiting around for ages. They told us to sit in Bruce Rioch's office, and wait for the 'Boro manager and the club secretary to come in and commence the talks.

"Bruce had a big cabinet behind his desk which was full of football programmes, all filed meticulously in date order. Bairdy, who gets bored easily, went to the cabinet and started to rearrange all the programmes, mixing up the order.

"The wait continued, the boredom had really set in and Bairdy was becoming quite edgy. He took his wedding ring off and started flicking it up in the air. He inevitably dropped it and it rolled under the desk. There he was, on all fours scrambling about to find the ring. I stood up, opened the door and slammed it shut, Bairdy went to get up and smacked his head on the underside of the table, dropping the ring again – at which point the club secretary walked in.

"When Rioch eventually entered his office, he instantly knew that Bairdy had been pissing around with his programmes and he gave him one hell of a look. As much as we tried to be professional, it was a laugh a minute with Bairdy and everywhere we went I knew that there would be some sort of incident.

"He often played the fool, but he is a wise lad who generally knew what he wanted and how to get it. But I was there to step in if the situation got tense or any disputes arose. The last thing we wanted was for him to get off to a bad start with his new employers."

Ian eventually signed for Middlesbrough in a deal worth £500,000, despite failing two medicals:

"I had to undergo a stringent medical and the doctor came back twice and told Rioch of a problem with my ankle. I had suffered with ankle problems, and I'd got by with those cortisone injections and strappings.

"In the end Bruce told the doctor not to mention it on his report. He had looked at my career statistics, and knew that it wasn't a problem that had caused me to miss games. He wanted me to sign and it didn't concern him.

"Trevor Putney was one of the first lads I spoke to. Trevor had moved north after playing his football in East Anglia. He told me that the place was unreal, and things happened up at Middlesbrough that he'd never experienced before."

Baird had swopped a promotion battle for a fight to stay in the league. 'Boro, to the surprise of many, were struggling and there was a real possibility of consecutive relegations,

"I walked into a dressing room which was full of great lads and very good football players – the likes of Stephen Pears, Colin Cooper, Simon Coleman, Bernie Slaven, Mark Proctor, Paul Kerr, Peter Davenport, Stuart Ripley, Gary Parkinson, Trevor Putney and Tony Mowbray. However, confidence was low and as a result the club was in a false position as far as the league table was concerned."

Baird made his debut at Ayresome Park on the 3rd of February 1990, with the club 19th in the league table going into the game. Goals from Paul Kerr and Bernie Slaven ensured a 2-0 win against one of his former clubs, Portsmouth, in front of 15,295.

"At half-time I began to understand what Putney meant. Slaven and Rioch had a disagreement and they started fighting. They were going at it hammer and tongs. Putney was sat at the side of me and whispered, 'I told you, they're fucking mental up here.'"

In a game that produced very few goal-scoring opportunities, Ian had a fairly quiet debut, although he was involved in the build-up which saw Bernie Slaven seal a welcome three points with the second goal eight minutes into the second half.

Slaven was a prolific goal-scorer who was idolised by the Middlesbrough faithful, and he looks back at his time partnering Ian Baird in the 'Boro attack with great fondness:

"Bairdy was the best centre-forward I ever played with at Middlesbrough. He was generally a quiet character who was a fantastic player. He displayed some nice touches and would run all day. On top of that, he certainly could handle himself."

The win over Portsmouth lifted Middlesbrough three places in the league but it would be a further seven games before they tasted another victory, by which time they found themselves in real trouble at the bottom end of the league.

One defeat came on the south coast, at Brighton & Hove Albion. The night before was spent in the Grand Hotel and Simon Coleman remembers an incident involving Baird:

"Bruce Rioch was sat in reception, talking to Colin Todd and the kit man. After witnessing one or two of the lads having a few beers, he ordered them to their rooms to get some sleep. Ian retired to his room as he was told. But he had other ideas and telephoned reception to order two pints.

"A few minutes later there was a knock and Bairdy jumped off the bed to open the door, only to be greeted by the kit man who stood there with two empty pint glasses."

Ian and Simon had struck up a good relationship off the field, and the defender openly admits that Baird was a big influence on his own career:

"We became good mates, and Ian often stayed at my house rather than travel back to his home in South Yorkshire after a night out. He was a proper lad and was a massive influence on my career. Play hard, work hard was Ian's method. He gave his all and would never switch off.

"Nights out were always eventful, there was never a dull moment with Ian. After one midweek game, Bairdy, Gary Parkinson and I went to a restaurant/

club in town that didn't close until six o'clock in the morning. Bairdy was giving the waitress some stick, and she didn't appreciate it.

"The following day she telephoned the club and got the word to the management that we had been out all night. Needless to say, a severe bollocking came our way when we reported for training, and Bairdy was ordered back to the establishment to apologise to the young lady he had offended."

Despite starting in every game since his move from Leeds United, Ian had yet to register a goal. But he wasn't the only one struggling to put the ball in the net. Just one goal had been scored in five games, coming from Simon Coleman in a 2-1 defeat against Watford which proved to be the final game of Rioch's tenure.

The man who had signed Ian was sacked on the 9th of March, to be replaced by his assistant Colin Todd. Baird was sorry to see Bruce leave:

"Bruce Rioch was a good guy, who everyday would be clean shaven and always dressed immaculately. A bit of an old-school character, but I enjoyed working for him. Training was enjoyable, and looking back I wish I had played for him a bit longer.

"When Todd came in, we were just weeks away from a Wembley cup final. And although we knew there was some hard work ahead, particularly in the league, things seemed more relaxed."

The eight-game goal drought ended for Baird on the 20th of March against Plymouth Argyle, a club he always seemed to score against. It came in the 37th minute of a 2-1 win, with Mark Brennan claiming the other goal:

"It was nice to get off the mark in a 'Boro shirt. I anticipated a poor back pass from the Argyle defender Andy Morrison and drove the ball past the goalkeeper. It set us on the way to a vital win, which gave the lads a big confidence boost going into the Wembley final. But more importantly it was three points in the battle to avoid the drop."

Five days later, Middlesbrough faced First Division side Chelsea in the final of the Zenith Data Systems Cup. It was a game that Baird was forced to sit out as he was cup-tied, having played for Leeds United in the earlier rounds. He also received an unexpected bonus from the Football Association:

"Due to an accumulation of bookings, I had received a one-match suspension. But the FA confirmed that the ban would be served by missing the final – despite the fact I was ineligible to play in the game anyway.

"I couldn't believe it; the suits in the ivory towers of the Football Association had done me a huge favour rather than hammer me like they had in the past."

Following the victory at Plymouth, 'Boro stayed in some obscure retreat near Devon as they prepared for the cup final. It was a strange situation for Bairdy, who had recently joined the club and had played no part in the cup run:

"Gary Hamilton was injured – and due to me being cup-tied, we were the only two who wouldn't be part of the squad at Wembley, and we whiled the week away playing snooker and having a few beers.

"We travelled to Wembley on the Friday, and I received a call informing me that Lesley had been taken to hospital. We were expecting our second child and there had been some complications.

"The bus dropped me off at Heathrow Airport, and I hired a car and drove up to Sheffield to be at Lesley's side. Thankfully all turned out well, but the Zenith Data Systems Cup Final was the last thing on my mind that weekend."

# 14

# Donkey ears and mixed emotions

Chelsea won the game 1-0 and from then on in, 'Boro's league form remained inconsistent. But Baird and Slaven's partnership up front really started to gel and the goals were flowing.

On the 11th of April, Peter Davenport scored the second goal in an entertaining 3-2 defeat at Port Vale. From that point, Middlesbrough scored nine times in the remaining seven games: Slaven hit five of them, whilst Baird knocked in the other four.

After a run of four games without a win, the club was in the bottom three. On the final day of the season they faced rivals Newcastle United, knowing anything but a win would see them relegated. They were also relying on league leaders Leeds United, themselves going for the title, not losing at Bournemouth – who were battling with Middlesbrough to avoid relegation. At the top and bottom these games were crucial, and there were many permutations.

Newcastle United were in third place, and needed a victory to have any hope of winning automatic promotion. It was an incredibly tense afternoon. Ayresome Park was bathed in sunshine, the atmosphere was electric and the players knew they had to deliver.

As expected, the game was a hotly contested north-east derby and the teams, with so much at stake, returned to the dressing rooms at half-time with the game goalless but not lacking incident. After one early altercation, Baird feared he would have to come off, when he went down injured in the first minute after a challenge by Roy Aitken. But thankfully he was able to run the effects off and carry on.

The match exploded into life after 60 minutes – and nobody could have predicted what was to follow as Baird and Bernie Slaven turned on the style, buoyed by news filtering through from Dean Court:

"The ground went mental just before we scored our first goal when it became apparent that Leeds had gone in front down at Bournemouth."

Within six minutes of Lee Chapman's header on the south coast, Middlesbrough took the lead in a pulsating clash through Slaven, then 1-0 quickly became 2-0 in the 66th minute when Baird made his mark:

"John Anderson attempted to head the ball back to his goalkeeper, John Burridge. Bernie capitalised and put the ball across the face of the goal. I was practically stood on the goal line and couldn't miss."

Of all the goals Ian scored in his career, he never had an easier one. But that can't be said of his second strike, just nine minutes later:

"It was 2-1 by then, Owen McGee had scored an own goal. We were in possession, and Mark Proctor played the ball through and I latched onto it before cracking a rising shot past Burridge in front of the Holgate End."

It was a goal fit to put the seal on any game, but things got even better when Slaven scored his second and 'Boro's fourth with only a minute to go. The superb 4-1 victory, coupled with the news that Leeds had beaten Bournemouth, ensured that jubilant scenes were witnessed at Ayresome Park as 'Boro knew they had avoided the drop .

During the game, there was an incident involving Baird and the Newcastle central defender Kevin Scott that went down in Middlesbrough folklore. To this day it is still discussed widely on social media sites and message boards:

"Kevin Scott was a centre-half with whom I'd enjoyed many battles over the years. We were in total control of the game and attacking the Holgate. I was shielding the ball, and he came straight through and clattered me. I picked myself up and gave him the 'Donkey ears sign'. Kevin wasn't happy and there were a few expletives exchanged. I enjoyed it, I didn't like any opponent during the game and I knew I had got to him that day."

The afternoon could not have gone any better for Ian. Not only had he helped his current club retain their status in the second tier, he had also picked up a Second Division title winners medal following his former club's victory at Dean Court:

"I was shattered that night, mentally and physically. I called in at my local where I had a couple of pints, and then went home for some much needed rest and a very early night whilst most of the Middlesbrough lads were out on the town. I was obviously pleased with my performance and the two goals and I was ecstatic that we had stayed up. But I couldn't help but let my mind wander, and think what could have been as my old club was winning the league.

"I will admit it was tough seeing pictures of the Leeds players celebrating with the trophy, and receiving the adulation of the fans that had craved the success for so long. I didn't begrudge them. I was thrilled, but even to this day it is still hard to understand why I acted in such a stupid fashion. I was chasing money, and committed the cardinal sin of leaving a club that was about to take off. It was tough.

"To be fair to Leeds United, they were brilliant with me. They ensured I received my championship medal, and they also paid me my promotion bonus which Hayden had negotiated."

In addition, a select group of Leeds fans had decided that they would hold their own independent Player of the Year awards night. A few players – including Baird and Bobby Davison along with their partners – were invited to a black-tie evening held at Linton Springs, a plush hotel and restaurant in Wetherby. Hayden Evans and a few other businessmen chipped in to pay for the venue:

"One of the conditions of us hiring that particular venue was that they would not close the bar until everybody had gone to bed. It was the early hours and there were Bairdy, Bobby and I left in the bar when one of the barmen started to pull the shutters down.

"Bairdy, who we could see was ready to go off on one, started to argue with the barman and ended up outside. Bobby, who was ready to wind Bairdy up even more, closed the door and Bairdy couldn't get back in.

"The following morning we came down from our rooms to discover that the Old Bill wanted us to report to Wetherby police station, as apparently various acts of vandalism had been carried out.

"The three of us were released with a warning. And although I was self-employed, I was called into Elland Road along with Bobby, and received a bollocking from Howard Wilkinson. Saying that, it was nothing to what we received when got home to our partners."

# 15

# More play-off despair

Despite the regrets of hastily ending his own Leeds career, Baird knew he couldn't change the past and was fully committed to Middlesbrough's cause. In an attempt to avoid the struggles of the previous season, manager Colin Todd had brought in the Scottish international John Wark, along with Robbie Mustoe and one of Ian's former team mates from Leeds United, John Hendrie,

"John Hendrie was a great signing, who I knew all about having played with him at Elland Road. John was a good guy, despite the fact he was always moaning. He would moan on the pitch and he would moan off the pitch, so much to the extent that he was christened 'Happy Hendrie'.

"I will always remember an incident during the 1990-91 season, when Hendrie was substituted at half-time. John wasn't happy and he told Colin Todd to 'fuck off'. Todd lunged forward and shoved John against the dressing room wall. To ensure the incident didn't boil over, John Wark and I pulled Todd off him and the situation calmed down."

A nice mix of youth and experience was evident at the club. One of the younger players, Alan Kernaghan is another who remains grateful for the influence of Ian Baird:

"Early on in my career, I sat with Ian on the team coach travelling to an away fixture. He told me how good I was and how I could influence the game. When we got in the dressing room, I felt ten foot tall. He was good like that, and I will always respect him."

Despite starting in the opening game of the season, Baird missed the following fixture at Plymouth Argyle. When he returned to the squad, he found himself on the substitute's bench before regaining his place on the 22$^{nd}$ of September at home to Oldham Athletic.

Middlesbrough had experienced an inconsistent start – winning two, drawing two and losing two of the opening six league games. But suddenly the team would find some good form, starting with a thumping 6-0 win over Leicester City. Baird scored the fifth goal that afternoon, which was his first of the season:

"I was up and running, the team were starting to play well and we were soon climbing up the league table. We travelled to Watford who were bottom and won 3-0. I managed to score twice that day, and then got another one in a 4-2 win at Brighton."

Ian had hit a purple patch in front of goal, and he found the net seven times in his next seven games – including a hat-trick in a stunning 5-2 win at Oxford United on the 24$^{th}$ of November.

The first came after only three minutes, when Hendrie was brought down just outside the box. John Wark took the free kick, and an unmarked Baird met it with a bullet header which went in off the underside of the bar. It was 2-0 after 17 minutes thanks to Slaven, but at half-time the teams were all square.

Baird made it 3-2 in the 64$^{th}$ minute when he slammed home a penalty after being brought down by Ceri Evans. Then four minutes after Robbie Mustoe made it 4-2, the striker sealed the game with his hat-trick goal and second penalty of the afternoon after Slaven had been fouled.

It was a proud moment for Ian, and the recent good run the club had been on had lifted them into the promotion race. It was a stark contrast to the previous season's struggles.

After a 3-0 win over Hull City – and another goal for Ian – Middlesbrough found themselves with no fixture the following weekend, and the club had arranged for the players to spend a few days in Playa De Las Americas:

"We flew out to Tenerife for a midseason break, and a few of the lads were intent on having a good time and enjoying it – especially the nightlife in Veronica's strip.

"Some of us were flat out on the piss for three or four days, from getting up to going to bed. However, nobody could actually believe the amount of booze that John Wark put away on that trip. It was incredible. I thought I could drink, but Warky was in a different league.

"We returned to the United Kingdom, and we were due to play West Ham United the following day. Soon after we had landed, Tony Mowbray pulled a few of us to one side and accused us of enjoying ourselves a little bit too much, and that he wouldn't be happy if we didn't perform well at Upton Park.

"Mowbray was Captain Sensible, and he was referred to as 'Victor Mature' after his comments. He was totally different to Warky who was far from Captain Sensible.

"Warky is a great lad, and he was a superb player who had been there, seen it and done it. He'd won countless trophies and awards and he brought so much quality to the club, but he certainly liked to enjoy himself off the field."

Remarkably, after the best part of a week propping up the bar and doing no training whatsoever, Middlesbrough battled their way to a 0-0 draw at Upton Park against the league leaders.

The second half of the season was disappointing. Although an Ian Baird goal at Ipswich Town on Boxing Day secured 'Boro a 1-0 win which sent them into third place, they would only win another eight games all season.

As a result the team limped over the line. They qualified for the play-offs on goal difference from Barnsley, but were some 13 points off Sheffield Wednesday who claimed the third automatic promotion spot.

Notts County were the opposition in the end-of-season lottery, and Baird admits that the play-offs came at the wrong time:

"We scraped in and our form wasn't good. We had lost four of the last six league games, and in those four defeats we failed to score a goal. It was complete contrast to Notts County, who had won their final seven matches."

The first leg at Ayresome Park ended all square, with Jimmy Phillips getting a late equaliser. But County won the second leg 1-0, and Middlesbrough were resigned to another season of Second Division football.

Several changes were made and they would start that new campaign without many of the current staff including the manager Colin Todd, and the popular centre-forward Ian Baird:

"I had been on holiday to Florida and a mate had picked me up from the airport when I arrived back in England. He delivered some news which I hadn't been expecting. Colin Todd had put me on the transfer list. I was staggered. I had a year left on my contract and had just been voted the club's player of the season.

"The first thing I did the following morning was to contact Todd. I told him I was upset about being transfer-listed. He informed me that it was a cost-cutting measure enforced by the club due to us missing out on promotion, and joining me on the list were Slaven, Wark, Cooper, Putney, Parkinson, McGee and Martin Russell."

Todd really stuck the boot in when he spoke to the media, advising them that he felt some of the players had not played to the best of their abilities and had let him down.

A few days later, the Middlesbrough board terminated Colin Todd's contract as manager of the club. He was replaced by the former Charlton Athletic boss Lennie Lawrence.

# 16

## Re-united with Joe

After much interest in Ian from clubs north of the border in 1987, and after Heart of Midlothian had a bid rejected a year later, Ian now had another chance to play his football in the Scottish Premier Division with the Tynecastle outfit.

Despite having one year remaining on his contract at Ayresome Park, the new Middlesbrough manager, Lennie Lawrence, said he would not stand in Ian's way if the chance of a move materialised. Baird was more than tempted when Joe Jordan declared an interest in taking him up to Edinburgh.

Bristol City were also keen on recruiting Ian Baird. They were managed at the time by Jimmy Lumsden, and the pair knew each other from their time at Elland Road,

"It had been very disappointing to be transfer-listed by Middlesbrough. I thoroughly enjoyed my time there and like at Leeds, I'd enjoyed a great relationship with the supporters but I saw there was yet another opportunity to make a few quid. I had spoken with Hearts and Bristol City – and eventually decided to join up with my old team mate, Joe Jordan, up in Scotland."

Joe was happy to get his man, but to do so he had to wheel and deal:

"When I negotiated the deal to sign Ian Baird, I was told there wasn't the money to pay for him. So before it could go through, I had to sell John Colquhoun. We had a good side and Ian fulfilled all expectations."

Back in Bristol, Jimmy Lumsden was far from happy at Baird's decision, informing him that he was making a huge mistake by going to Hearts. But the centre-forward's mind was made up,

"No disrespect to the Scottish Premier League now. But the standard was much higher back then, and the move enabled me to play alongside and test myself against some top class football players. But another deciding factor was the opportunity to work with Joe, who had been a big influence on me during our time together at The Dell. Whenever I see Jimmy Lumsden, he still reminds me that I should have signed for him when I left Middlesbrough.

"The negotiations were pretty straightforward, although I had to tell Hayden to get a grip as he was very nervous and in awe of Joe Jordan. Hayden was a young lad when Joe played for Leeds, and he idolised the Scottish international centre-forward.

"I was looking forward to a new challenge at Hearts, and it helped knowing that I was going to be part of a very good side which included Gary Mackay, Scott Crabbe, Alan McLaren, John Robertson, Craig Levein, Henry Smith, Dave McPherson and Tosh McKinlay. The majority of the lads were local and had supported the club throughout their childhood.

"The likes of Mackay and Robbo had been there for years, as had the physio Allan Rae. The youth team manager Sandy Clark had played for the club, and ex-players would always be around the place. It was a very close-knit unit, one big family.

"In reality, coming up from England I was an outsider, and it made a real impression on me seeing what the club meant to these lads. They loved it – especially Mackay and Crabbe, they were real diehards. I will always remember trips home from away games, the bus would be coming over the Forth Road Bridge and Mackay would proudly say, 'Welcome back to the capital city'."

That sense of pride and the togetherness was perhaps a key factor in Hearts going on to have such a tremendous season. In preparation for the new campaign, Baird scored his first goal for his new club in a pre-season friendly – at home to the Spanish side, Real Sociedad. It came from the penalty spot in the 72nd minute, just moments before he was substituted.

The competitive action got underway the following week. Hearts got their season off to the best possible start with a 2-1 victory away at Dunfermline Athletic, despite having Tosh McKinlay sent off. In the crowd that day was Hayden Evans, and he was quick to spot something he felt would be a key benefit to Baird:

"The referees were poor, and didn't know how to handle Bairdy or deal with his aggressive style of play. I told him afterwards, 'You should love it here, you'll get away with murder.'"

The point of view was echoed by Hearts legend and Scottish international forward John Robertson:

"Ian arrived at Hearts with a big reputation. His style of play was like that of Joe Jordan's. On the pitch and on the training ground, he was fully committed and never shirked a challenge. He was unplayable at times – Scottish football didn't have many strikers like Ian, very good in the air, possessed a great touch and was superb at holding the ball up.

"We would play keep-ball in training, and if ever Ian got nut-megged he would try and break your leg – he hated it, and I can remember a training-ground incident when he went in two-footed on Eammon Bannon. Eammon had been winding him up, that wasn't wise.

"There's a big stand at Tynecastle, and in the warm ups before games Bairdy would attempt to hammer the ball over the top of the stand. He never managed it, but on one occasion Alan McLaren did eventually and Bairdy was raging."

Hearts followed up their opening-day victory with a 3-2 win away at Airdrieonians. It was a game that saw Ian Baird notch his first competitive goal, when he forced the ball over the line following a goalmouth scramble in the 48th minute.

The club was flying and topped the table for large parts of the season. Baird was more than playing his part, having scored eight goals before the turn of the year. However, things would soon start to turn sour,

"We had gone 15 games unbeaten and during that run we had beaten Celtic twice. However, a week after we had won at Parkhead we were thumped 4-0 at home by Aberdeen, and some of the Hearts fans were throwing their scarves onto the pitch in disgust at the end of the game. I found that very strange."

With the club second in the league, two points behind Rangers, attentions turned to the Scottish Cup and a trip to St Mirren in round three. Love Street was a ground where Baird had received a red card earlier in the season and during the cup tie, which ended in a 0-0 stalemate, he got another one. The incident sent shockwaves through Scottish football,

"Chic Charnley was playing for St Mirren at the time, he had a reputation as a hard man in Scotland. I had a run-in with him and verbals were exchanged. The incident fired me up, and in the 71st minute I went up for a header with the goalkeeper, Campbell Money. The clash resulted in Money suffering a broken jaw – I put him and the ball into the net. The goal was disallowed and I received a straight red card.

"The pundits on Scottish television claimed that I should be outlawed from the game and my Uncle John, who I was living with at the time, refused to speak to me for months – claiming I had brought shame on Hearts, Scottish football and the family."

Baird served his ban, but soon after getting back in the side he suffered a torn thigh muscle. It forced him to miss more vital league games and also a Scottish Cup Semi-Final tie, against Airdrieonians at Hampden Park:

"We had fallen five points behind league leaders Rangers and sat in third place, level on points with Celtic. But we really fancied our chances of reaching the Scottish Cup Final. The game with Airdrie ended 0-0. I was gutted to miss out, but Joe brought me back for the replay ten days later.

"To be perfectly honest, I wasn't ready and should never have played. I was restricted due to the injury, and was substituted ten minutes into the second half. I took some criticism from sections of the Hearts supporters, but Joe had kept the injury quiet and that disappointed me a little."

Despite a late equaliser from Alan McLaren, Hearts eventually lost the tie in a penalty shoot-out. The league title dream was all but over, and so were the chances of cup glory.

"We had a relatively small squad and operated with around 15 players. Maybe it was down to finances that Joe was unable to strengthen key areas, but we fell away in the league title race. Rangers ran away with it in the end but it was nice to pip their old firm rivals, Celtic, into second place."

Due to the fact they finished runners-up, they had qualified for the UEFA Cup. As a result, the club rewarded the squad with a trip to Spain:

"As the season reached its business end, we were challenging at the top end of the league. I had laid off the booze for three months but that all changed when we landed in Spain. A few of us had already decided that we would go on a mission to drink solid for five days.

"Much of the trip was a blur as we got stuck into the booze, but I do remember a few incidents. On one of the nights we were in Manos bar in Magaluf. I was in the middle of a 24-hour non-stop alcohol binge, and things went a bit too far when Gary Mackay pissed into an ashtray and threw the contents over my head.

"Understandably, I didn't appreciate what Gary did and I went berserk. I threw myself at him and pinned him to the floor before we were separated. Gary soon apologised once we had sobered up, he knew he had been out of order and that was the end of the matter.

"Another incident occurred when I was so pissed that I had fallen asleep in the street outside a bar. Joe had found me, tapped me on the head and gave me the look which told me he wasn't best pleased.

"We were at the airport for the flight home later that night, and both Sandy Clark and Frank Connor had told me to expect a bollocking. I had a major hangover and just wanted to get home."

Ian was due to be picked up by Lesley at the airport when they landed. But Joe declared that he had to go with him, straight to Tynecastle.

The manager laid the law down, telling Baird that he'd never seen a professional footballer behave in that manner. Despite Ian's attempts to convince Joe, his excuses fell on deaf ears and he was severely reprimanded:

"I explained to Joe that although I may have gone over the top, I hadn't had a drink for three months. But he informed me that he thought my behaviour was outrageous, and that if I ever carried on like that in the future then I would never kick a ball for him again."

# 17

# Back between the sticks

Baird was loving life north of the border, and he had settled with his family in the Fairmilehead area of Edinburgh:

"It was a fantastic place to live. We had a lovely house and we were enjoying it up there. We had a great social scene – Gary Mackay, Tosh McKinlay, myself and our partners would often enjoy a night out. Also, along with John Robertson and a few others we would go to Morningside after a game and enjoy a few beers. Robbo was a legend there."

Despite the incident in Spain, which was soon forgotten about, Baird held Gary Mackay in high regard. The pair got on well, and the respect was mutual:

"We had a strange mix on the social side, but we had some good times. Bairdy loved a drink and would have an absolute skinful, whereas I would be wobbling on three shandies and Tosh was a staunch teetotal.

"It was all or nothing with Ian in anything he did – training, playing or socialising, and there were no grey areas. He had plenty of run-ins and fall-outs but they were soon resolved. If he had a problem with anybody in the dressing room, he would bring it to the fore and not dwell on any issues that bothered him, no matter how big or small."

Baird, along with Robertson and Scott Crabbe, formed a formidable front three. But he jokes it was tough playing beside the club's record goalscorer, Robertson:

"It wasn't enjoyable operating alongside Robbo. Over the course of my career at various clubs, I played alongside several strikers. But three of them – Micky Quinn at Portsmouth, Bernie Slaven at Middlesbrough and John

Robertson at Hearts – easily took six years off my career because I had to do all their running for them.

"Robbo was a poacher, a quality finisher and a top player. And although he never stopped talking about himself, he was a good lad and I thoroughly enjoyed his company.

"It was an honour to play in his testimonial game during the summer of 1992. We beat Kevin Keegan's Newcastle United side 1-0, and I was lucky enough to get the winner."

As the new season got underway, Baird was still struggling with the effects of the previous season's injury and he was finding life tough:

"Things didn't really go to plan for me. The injury was causing me a lot of trouble. I had to play because the squad was threadbare, Joe had limited options."

Just four days after scoring a late winner against Partick Thistle at Tynecastle, Baird came in for some terrible abuse from his own supporters:

"We played a League Cup tie, away to Second Division side Brechin City, and I had an absolute nightmare. I got slaughtered by a section of the Hearts fans that made up a crowd of just under 2,000 supporters. They were stood very close to the pitch at Brechin and one guy had been giving me abuse from the first whistle – and by the time I was substituted I had just about had enough, and made a bee-line for him.

"It was a good job that Frank Connor stepped in and defused the situation by pulling me away. Frank was old school, and a really good bloke who was always very supportive."

Once again, Hearts were performing well in the league and although they were eliminated from the League Cup by Celtic, the UEFA Cup was just around the corner.

By the time the Jambos travelled to the Czech Republic to play Slavia Prague in mid-September, they were second in the league – level on points with Rangers.

It was a tough place to go, especially with Craig Levein and Alan McLaren missing from the back four. But Hearts produced a spirited display before going down to a late goal scored by Vladimir Tatarchuk.

Two league defeats were suffered before the return leg at Tynecastle, which proved to be a memorable night as Hearts ran out 4-2 winners against the ten men of Slavia. Baird grabbed the second goal after 21 minutes when he headed home an Eammon Bannon cross, and with the tie delicately poised it was left to Glynn Snodin to fire home a 25-yard free kick with just 11 minutes remaining.

That goal sent Hearts into the second round, where they were beaten 1-0 in both legs against the Belgian outfit Standard Liege.

At the turn of the year, Joe Jordan's men found themselves in fourth place in the league, a massive ten points behind Rangers – leaving the Scottish Cup as their only realistic hope of lifting any silverware.

Non-league side Huntly were the visitors to Tynecastle in the third round, and Baird set Hearts on their way to a thumping 6-0 win. Dundee were beaten in the fourth round and Falkirk were disposed of in the quarter-final. This set up a semi-final tie with Rangers, who ran out 2-1 winners at Parkhead. Jordan's men had fallen at the semi-final stage for the second successive season.

Although the chase for any honours was over, there was plenty of drama in store – and Saturday the 17th of April was a day that Ian Baird will never forget.

Hearts travelled to Aberdeen's Pittodrie Stadium for a league fixture, and the bustling striker found himself playing an unfamiliar role:

"Nicky Walker, our number one, tore a leg muscle in the warm up. And with no substitute goalkeeper in those days, I volunteered to don the gloves. I had always enjoyed messing around between the sticks in training and had played there in my younger days. But this was a different kettle of fish, and I was the most nervous I'd ever been before a game in my life."

After 57 minutes, Hearts found themselves 3-0 down but Baird claimed that there was nothing that he could have done about any of the goals. Despite a brave Hearts fight back, they lost the game 3-2. After some harsh criticism from his manager, Baird admitted that he wouldn't be volunteering for that particular role should the situation arise in the future.

When it was suggested to Jordan that his stand-in goalkeeper had done a commendable job, he would only say, 'I suggest you look very carefully at the first and third goals.'"

It was very harsh criticism, and perhaps a sign that Joe knew the pressure was on. Following a 6-0 thrashing at Falkirk two weeks later, he was sacked and Sandy Clark was appointed as his replacement.

More drama followed against Aberdeen, this time at Tynecastle, when the linesman indicated that Baird had gestured to the fans after grabbing an equaliser. After consultation, the referee gave him a second yellow card and an early bath.

Despite this latest setback, Baird – or Yogi as he had become affectionately known – had won the fans over. His reward came at the end of the season when he was voted player of the year by the Heart of Midlothian Supporters Club, which was no mean feat for an Englishman:

"It was nice to win the award. I was over moon and it showed that I had proved the doubters and the boo-boys wrong.

"My contract was up and despite the fact that Sandy Clark was prepared to offer me a new deal, I knew that clubs in England were interested in me. I went off on holiday and made a decision that I would return south."

# 18

## A collapsed lung and broken ribs

Ian's decision to leave Tynecastle in July 1993 was based on personal reasons and, having just bought a new house on the outskirts of Southampton, he wanted to be nearer home. Leicester City had shown interest, but Bristol City presented Ian with a great opportunity:

"I spoke to Leicester but Bristol City was my preferred option. I knew Russell Osman, who was the manager at the time, from my days at Southampton and he was a real football man who had been a great player.

"In addition, Bristol was only a 90-minute drive from my home so I was able to commute. We agreed a deal and the fee involved, £285,000, was settled by a tribunal. I was keen to get started, despite the fact there were problems at the club which had begun before I had walked through the door.

"The atmosphere wasn't the best, and there were players who knew they were on their way out of Ashton Gate. Russell Osman wanted to get rid of the likes of Mark Aizlewood, Nicky Morgan, Mark Gavin and Gary Shelton and this created a real divide in the dressing room. In addition there was a real drinking culture, which was on a different level to anything I'd experienced before.

"We travelled to Ireland for a pre-season tour and certain members of the squad were out every night – and one morning I went down for breakfast at 7:30 and some of them were still in the bar.

"Whilst in Ireland we played three friendlies, against Cobh Ramblers, Limerick and Galway. All three games were won and I grabbed my first goal for the club in the 3-2 win over Limerick.

"Russell signed a few players around the same time that I had joined. Liam Robinson came in who was a great lad, and another was a guy called Dave Martin who I became good friends with.

"In truth though, Dave did himself no favours from the start. When joining a new club you want to do your best, keep your nose clean and give a good impression. But Dave ended up mixing with the lads in Ireland who were constantly out on the piss."

Ian got off to a flying start at Ashton Gate, with a goal in a 2-0 win over Crystal Palace on his home debut. It was the first of five goals before the end of October, when he faced a spell on the sidelines:

"In addition to suffering with an Achilles injury, I needed a hernia operation and didn't return to action until the Christmas period when I came on as a substitute against West Bromwich Albion. I started on the bench the following day, at home to Nottingham Forest, and was back in the starting line-up for the New Year's Day fixture at Grimsby Town.

"Despite some indifferent results in the league, the place was buzzing as we had drawn Liverpool in the FA Cup at Ashton Gate. Everybody was looking forward to the occasion."

Unfortunately for Ian, he was about to pick up a serious injury which would all but finish his season:

"We played Stoke City at home, and just before half-time I chased a through ball. In doing so I collided with the opposition goalkeeper, Gordon Marshall, and instantly I knew something was wrong.

"I received treatment in the dressing room at half-time and came out for the second half. But as the game continued, the pain increased and it was difficult to breathe. I should never have gone out for the second half but I did, and I played through the pain barrier before being substituted in the dying moments of the game.

"A mate of mine was at the game and he drove me straight home. The pain was getting worse and it was becoming harder to breathe. I couldn't eat anything and eventually, early on the following morning, Lesley had to take me to the hospital. I was in absolute agony."

Ian was admitted into intensive care, where he was diagnosed with five broken ribs and a collapsed lung. He received anaesthetic and the lung had to be re-inflated.

"It was very frustrating, having just regained my fitness following the hernia operation and the Achilles trouble. I was back into the team, I was enjoying my football and it didn't take a genius to realise that I had no chance of playing against Liverpool.

"I was resting at home and, unbelievably, the situation became worse when it transpired that the lung had become infected and I had to spend a further two and a half weeks in the hospital."

Bristol City's original tie with Liverpool was abandoned after 65 minutes due to floodlight failure, with the scores level at 1-1. When the two sides tried again, the Premier League outfit were lucky to escape with a draw and were hanging on after Wayne Allison levelled matters following Ian Rush's opener.

The replay at Anfield was a truly memorable night for Bristol City – on which they produced one of the great cup shocks, courtesy of a stunning 66th-minute goal scored by Brian Tinnion. The Robins had eliminated a star-studded Liverpool line-up, in a game that would prove to be Graeme Souness' last in charge of the Merseyside club.

It wasn't until March that Baird returned to match fitness, and he made his first team comeback as a substitute at home to Portsmouth:

"I was obviously pleased to be back. But during a reserve game a few days later I took a knock in the ribs, it was the same spot where I had collided with Marshall. We were due to play Bolton Wanderers on the Saturday and I travelled with the squad up to Manchester, where we stayed overnight.

"On the morning of the game I woke up with the shakes. I was sweating profusely and was unable to climb out of bed. My room-mate Liam Robinson had to go and get Osman and the physiotherapist to come and see me."

Fortunately for Ian, the manager had taken his own car up to Lancashire. After the game, he drove Baird straight back to Bristol and to a private hospital where he was admitted straightaway.

It was yet another blow for Ian Baird, and one that would bring his season to an end:

"I had picked up another infection, this time in one of my ribs, and it required an operation. Three quarters of the affected rib was cut out – resulting in another spell laid up in hospital, this time for two weeks."

Due to the fact that Ian couldn't play or train, he decided to take a break and travelled to New York with Lesley for a long weekend:

"Osman wasn't happy that I went to New York, and he made a point of telling me so. We had words, and I explained that if the injury had been correctly diagnosed by the club then I wouldn't have gone out in the second half against Stoke and attempted to play with five broken ribs and a collapsed lung. In addition, as a result of the injury and through no fault of my own, I had missed out on bonus payments.

"To be fair to him he went to the board of directors and, following a bit of fuss, I was eventually paid the bonuses that I believed I was more than entitled to."

During his lengthy lay-off, Baird had shed a stone-and-a-half in weight. But as soon as he got the thumbs up to return to training, his focus was on getting himself into shape and regaining his fitness in time for the new campaign.

# 19

# In trouble at Ashton Gate

Ian Baird was back in the side as Bristol City's 1994-95 season got underway with a goalless draw at home to Sunderland. City kept a clean sheet the following week at Bolton Wanderers, when they came away with all three points as strike partners Allison and Baird claimed a goal each in an impressive 2-0 victory.

Wayne Allison, nicknamed The Chief, admits he benefited from playing alongside Ian, who he respects as a player and as a person:

"I have a tremendous amount of respect for Ian Baird. He would constantly talk to me throughout the game, offering his advice. He taught me how to conduct myself, how to stand up for myself and not be bullied by the opposition.

"Ian was a great player, with a fantastic touch and an eye for goal. At Bristol, all the play would go through Ian and he would battle away whilst I picked up the loose balls. He also had a nasty edge, and on some occasions his reputation did him no favours.

"When I left Ashton Gate and joined Swindon Town, I tried to put into practice everything that Bairdy had taught me. And there is no doubt that after the experience of playing alongside him, my game had improved and I became a better player."

Bristol City, despite starting the season fairly well, became very inconsistent and the pressure was building on Russell Osman. A heavy 5-1 defeat at Ashton Gate at the hands of Wolverhampton Wanderers, in which Ian scored City's goal, would be Osman's last home game in charge:

"Russell knew that he was under pressure, and a few days later we were beaten 3-0 at Brammall Lane by Sheffield United. On the journey back to Bristol, one of the lads on the coach asked Osman – who always mixed with players – about his position. He replied telling him that of course the pressure was on, but he didn't think that the club could afford to sack him."

Sack him they did, and the board acted swiftly in appointing Joe Jordan as the new manager. Baird was re-united with his mentor.

Ian was suspended due to a number of bookings when Joe arrived, and not available for selection. Joe won his first game in charge but lost the next six, and Bristol City were in serious trouble at the wrong end of the table. Jordan recognised that urgent changes were needed, and experienced Sunderland midfielder Gary Owers was brought to the club. Owers knew all about Baird having played against him many times:

"Ian Baird took no prisoners on or off the pitch and it was nice to have him on my side, but from the day I walked into Bristol City Football Club I sensed a weird atmosphere. Bairdy and Dave Martin ruled the roost in the dressing room and the banter was relentless – at times ferocious, often getting personal and aimed at wives and girlfriends.

"Although Ian liked to enjoy himself now and then, he was a great professional and you knew he would be the first one into training every morning. He would be at the front during the cross country runs, and would do extra work in the gym. Ian wouldn't accept anything less than 100% and one particular incident on the training ground, involving the ex-England coach John Gorman, sticks in my mind,

"John was Joe Jordan's assistant, and he was one of the nicest men that you could ever wish to meet in football. He would often join in at the start of training sessions, and one morning we were in a circle passing the ball about with Bairdy in the middle attempting to win possession.

"Everyone was on their toes and all of a sudden a short ball was played to John. I envisaged what would happen next. Bairdy took off – he was in mid-air, almost horizontal. He cut through Gorman at waist height, like a knife through butter. The place went deadly silent and it was almost like time had frozen. John was in tatters, laid on the grass and when he eventually picked himself up he could hardly walk. Bairdy had hold of the ball and shouted to Gorman to hurry up as it was his turn in the middle."

Dave Martin also recalled the Gorman incident. He admits that if he came up against Baird in practice games on the training ground, the two wouldn't hold back and any challenges would be made with full commitment:

"He was brilliant was Bairdy, he's the type of lad you want in the trenches with you. We were out one night on a Christmas party, and some Bristol Rovers fans took a dislike to me and there was plenty of tension. Eventually it all spilled outside, but Ian stood with me, he never showed any fear in any type of situation."

One of Joe Jordan's problems at the club was a lack of firepower. Bristol City had scored just four goals in nine games, three of them coming in a victory over Stoke City. To address the problem, Robert Fleck was signed on a three-month loan from Chelsea, and unfortunately for Ian that signalled a spell on the substitute's bench:

"Flecky was brought in to try and rescue Bristol City's season and although I was disappointed to be dropped, I could understand Joe's reasons. Fleck was a Scottish international who had been a hero at Norwich City and Glasgow Rangers, but he'd struggled at Chelsea, despite being their record signing at the time. He was a great lad off the field. But on the field he hardly improved the side, scoring one goal in ten starts."

The loan man was ineligible to play in the FA Cup, and Ian was back in the side for a third round replay away at Stoke City. The game would see The Robins progress in the tournament courtesy of a 3-1 victory, with Ian getting himself on the score sheet. However, Gary Owers remembers an incident in the changing room at half-time:

"It was a big game for us that Joe, on his return to the Potteries, was desperate to win. It has always been quite an intimidating place to go, and we knew we would be in for a battle.

"During the first half, Ian was holding the ball up, looking to lay it off to Vergard Hansen who hid behind an opponent and for some reason didn't appear to want the ball.

"Bairdy was absolutely seething when he got into the dressing room at half-time. I had never seen him so angry. He was like a raging bull, due to the fact that he gave his all and he expected the same in return. Anything less was unacceptable and rightly so.

"He launched a verbal attack on Hansen, who generally was a good lad and clearly didn't expect the bollocking he got. Let's just say, Hansen never let the situation happen again."

On the 18th of March, Ian started a league game for the first time since early January. Just three days later, he would play the hero and the villain in an away fixture at Notts County's Meadow Lane.

Ian gave City the lead in the 62nd minute. But he would not see the game out as he was sent off just seven minutes after his goal, having received a second booking for a foul on defender and ex-team-mate Graeme Hogg.

Ian returned to action as a substitute in the away game at Watford. City were beaten 1-0. The result confirmed that the following season they would be playing in the Second Division, which was the equivalent of League One today.

In a long career it was the only time that Ian Baird tasted the bitter pill of relegation:

"It was difficult for a lot of us. But the rot had well and truly set in and as the season reached the 'business end', the players knew that relegation was a formality.

"As a footballer you know when the writing is on the wall. We never gave up, of course we didn't, but you get that feeling. The chances we were missing and the late goals we were conceding. Things just weren't happening for us, and any club at the bottom of any league never gets the rub of the green.

"We had a good set of lads – Martin Kuhl, Mark Shail, Martin Scott, Junior Bent, The Chief, Brian Tinnion and Gary Owers, to name a few – but we didn't produce as a group."

Preparations for the new season and life in a lower division were underway and during pre-season, just six days before the big kick-off, Bristol City welcomed Ruud Gullit's Chelsea to Ashton Gate for a friendly. Events that day would all but end Ian Baird's Bristol City career:

"It was a typical pre-season friendly, played on a red hot day. A decent crowd turned up as expected due to the quality of the opposition.

"We were losing 1-0 to a John Spencer goal and after an hour I somehow failed to hit the target from a yard out, when I tried to sweep home a cross from Scott Partridge but the ball hit my standing foot.

"The miss was bad, I will hold my hands up. But the reaction, in a friendly, was ridiculous. The crowd went mental and I was getting dog's abuse, but I reacted in the worst possible way by flicking the bird towards the Bristol City faithful.

"Straight away Joe took me off the field. I was suspended by the club, told to stay away and I was placed on the transfer list. He had no option and I fully understood that."

Despite becoming 'Mr Unpopular' in the eyes of the Ashton Gate support, team-mate, Richard Dryden admits that Ian's presence around the club and in the changing room was missed by the majority of his colleagues:

"Bairdy was very lively and whilst he was away, a big part of the changing room went missing. He would always sit with Dave Martin – the two of them would be in the corner facing the door and they would absolutely hammer you as soon as you walked in, especially if you dared to wear any clothing that they didn't like. The key was to try and get in there before them and try and give them a bit of stick before they started on you.

"I felt that Bairdy got a rough deal from the Bristol supporters at times. He could control the ball three times and lay it off, but then the fourth time the ball would bounce of his shin, and the fans would be moaning and groaning and getting on his back.

"His knowledge of football is second to none and, although he would often act the clown to get a few laughs, he is a very intelligent guy."

Bristol City had a terrible start to their life in the Second Division, winning just one of their first seven games and scoring only four goals in the process. As a result, Baird was asked to return:

"I got a telephone call from John Gorman asking me if I would come back and play, due to the fact that they were struggling for results.

"Of course I wanted to play, and I returned to action on the 23rd of September 1995 in a 2-2 draw against Notts County. However, my situation at the club was untenable – and with Plymouth Argyle showing an interest in me, it was only a matter of time before I was back on my travels."

# 20

# Promoted with Warnock

Ian Baird arrived at Plymouth Argyle – a club he had always done well against – having accepted that following the incident in the friendly game, his days at Ashton Gate were numbered:

"I had to accept that I had no future at Bristol City, and I'd had a few conversations with Neil Warnock about the possibility of moving to Home Park to play for his Plymouth side. Warnock told me that he wanted to bring me in to me help get them promoted although I wouldn't start every game.

"I admired his honesty and, despite a sticking point over my wage which was eventually sorted, we agreed a deal and I was happy to sign."

Plymouth had made some big signings and they were the bookmakers' favourites for promotion. But they got off to the worst possible start, losing their first six games – four of them in the league – and both legs of a League Cup tie against Birmingham City.

Although things improved considerably, Warnock's assistant Mick Jones explained why they had brought Baird to the club:

"We brought Ian to Plymouth to win us promotion. We wanted a leader, and we knew he would score goals and create chances for others. He was a real man in the dressing room who didn't suffer fools. He only accepted maximum effort."

Ian made his debut for Plymouth Argyle at home to Lincoln City. He almost made a cracking start to life at Home Park but a header at goal came back off the cross bar:

"I enjoyed my debut, it was a game which we won 3-0. Argyle had some good players, including Micky Heathcote, Keith Hill, Adrian Littlejohn and Micky

Evans. There was a good team spirit which Warnock created and, although he wasn't everybody's cup of tea, people wanted to play for him.

"In a way the club was run like a Sunday league side. The training kit was tatty but that was Neil's style."

The following week Baird scored twice in another 3-0 home win, this time against Fulham. His first came with a cracking shot from the edge of the box and the second was another quality strike, direct from a free-kick.

Baird had brought a new dimension to Argyle's attack, and he was certainly making an impression on his new colleagues as he settled into life in the old Fourth Division. One of those colleagues, goalkeeper Kevin Blackwell, spoke fondly of Baird:

"Neil had been looking for an experienced striker, and Bairdy fitted the bill. He was a larger than life character who brought experience and quality to the side. He was very knowledgeable about the game, and I learnt aspects of football from him which I took into my coaching and management career."

At the end of October, the fixture list provided Argyle with two away games in a week – at Darlington on the Saturday and Scarborough on the Tuesday night,

"After the game at Darlington we made the trip across to the seaside town of Scarborough where we were staying over. Neil Warnock stayed in the best hotel that the place could offer, while the rest of us had to pay a tenner each to camp down in some very ropey guest house.

"One good thing about the trip, or so I thought, was that Warnock let us have a night out on the Saturday. As usually happens when big groups go out, people get split up, and towards the end of the night I was stood in a bar with Keith Hill.

"Keith and I had become close friends and socialised on a regular basis while at Plymouth. Keith's wife was back in Rochdale and he was staying in digs, while I commuted from Southampton but would often stay over.

"As we moved from pub to pub I had the feeling we were being followed, but 'Hilly' dismissed my concerns.

"We decided that we would round the night off by going for a curry. We were pissed up, and the restaurant owner thought better about letting us in. As we turned away to go back to the guest house, the same group of blokes who I thought were following us came steaming in. Keith got knocked out and I was on the floor, curled up in a ball while they kicked the shit out of me.

"The restaurant owner heard the commotion, came outside and threatened to call the Old Bill. It was a good job he did, as the lads scarpered leaving us in a bloodied mess on the floor.

"I needed six stitches in an eye wound and although Keith had been knocked out, we were very lucky. The next morning we had to explain ourselves to the management, but Keith shouldered the blame and told Warnock he had instigated the situation and it was his fault.

"I got the impression that Warnock dismissed Keith's claims, as he started Hilly against Scarborough and I was dropped to the bench."

The fun in Scarborough didn't end there, and it was proving to be a totally eventful experience for Ian for all the wrong reasons:

"Warnock brought me on with 15 minutes to go when we were leading 2-1. In the final minute of injury time, I committed a foul on the halfway line. From the free-kick, they put the ball straight into the mixer and equalised with the scrappiest goal you've ever seen.

"In the dressing room after the final whistle, all hell broke loose and Warnock went for me. He was shouting and screaming like a mad-man. I wanted to have a ruck with him, but it was probably for the best that Jonah pulled me away.

"There were no grudges afterwards as I knew that was Warnock's way. He was very passionate and he knew that I was very passionate."

Despite the dropped points by the seaside, results were picking up and Plymouth were climbing the league table. Baird was enjoying his football, and on a personal level the New Year got off to a great start with two goals in two games.

"I scored in a Devon derby at home to Exeter City – a game which we drew 2-2 – before a huge game for the club in the FA Cup against Coventry City, who were then in the Premier League."

On a day of gale force winds, the atmosphere inside a packed Home Park was electrifying. With the score at 0-0, Argyle's Mickey Evans was brought down by David Busst, and hopes of a cup shock were enhanced when the Sky Blues defender was shown a straight red card.

Baird raised those hopes to another level when he took the resulting free-kick and hammered the ball into the top corner of Steve Ogrizovic's goal, putting the home side into a 1-0 lead. It was a fantastic strike although Ian, in his modesty, claims it was wind-assisted.

Unfortunately, Coventry's Premier League class shone through in the end, and three quick goals in the second half killed any hopes of Argyle progressing at the expense of their Premier League opponents.

Baird grabbed further goals in a draw at home to Colchester United and a win at Cambridge United. But then a groin injury, suffered in the 20th minute of a 4-0 thrashing at Fulham on the 30th of March, would just about end his season.

"I had been suffering with a groin problem, and I went out to face Fulham having had three cortisone injections to ensure I was ready. It took me a while to recover from this latest setback and, although I made the bench towards the very end of the season, I never kicked another ball during that campaign."

Plymouth battled on without their influential striker and the club finished the regular season in fourth place, which earned them a place in the play-offs.

Ian was working his way back to fitness, and wasn't present at the first leg of the semi-final when Plymouth lost at Colchester United's Layer Road ground by a single goal:

"Warnock had told me to stay at home and rest, so that I could be ready for the second leg. He wanted me on the bench, saying it would give Argyle a psychological advantage if the Colchester back four knew I was waiting to come on. Whether that's true or not, I wouldn't like to say, but it was Warnock's way of making you feel good about yourself which raised confidence levels."

A big crowd turned up at Home Park to see if Plymouth could overturn the 1-0 defeat in the first leg. They didn't go home disappointed, as goals from Mickey Evans, Chris Leadbitter and Paul Williams ensured a 3-1 win on the night and a trip to Wembley.

Prior to the play-off final, the Plymouth management, staff and players enjoyed a few days in the stunning surroundings of The Belfry. But what was supposed to be relaxing break ended with Ian, once again, facing the wrath of Neil Warnock:

"Keith Hill, Gary Patterson and I had been out on the golf course and played a three-ball. Hilly was never the greatest golfer in the world but we enjoyed the game. Once back in the bar, we hit the Stella. Patterson was sensible and only had a couple of pints, while Keith and I really got stuck into it and then had a bottle of red wine.

"Red wine and Stella is never a good combination and we were absolutely steaming. The drink continued to flow and I suggested that we carry on and go to a night club – but Micky Heathcote, the club captain, advised us to go and get some sleep.

"I wasn't interested in what Heathcote suggested, and I didn't appreciate being told what to do. Inevitably, words were exchanged, Warnock got involved, and I ended up telling a few people at the club what I thought of them."

Ian stayed in the bar, contemplating his next move, but the rest of the night became a blur. The following morning when he went downstairs for breakfast, there was an awkward silence as he walked into the dining area:

"Everybody was quiet and I could feel the tension. It was obvious the word had got round about the incident in the bar, and Warnock was far from happy. Norman Medhurst, the physiotherapist, then ordered me to go up and see Neil in his room.

"The manager was waiting and he told me in no uncertain terms, 'Pack your bags. I am not having you talk to me like you did and behave the way you did last night. In my role of being the manager of Plymouth Argyle, I have to be seen to take some action. Get in your car, go home and you won't be involved at Wembley.'"

Ian – suffering with a major hangover – did as he was ordered, pulling into the hard shoulder on the motorway and having three hours' sleep.

Two days later Ian reported for training, where he got his head down and worked hard as the club prepared for its big day at Wembley. Mick Jones spoke to Ian about the incident and couldn't believe his response:

"Bairdy had crossed the line, and I asked him what he was playing at. He pleaded that it wasn't him, it was his twin – and when he's had a drink his twin takes over.

"I'd heard some excuses but that was a classic. I relayed to Neil that Bairdy had a twin. He didn't see the funny side and wasn't sure who was the taking the piss, me or Ian."

Despite the incident in the hotel, and the fact he'd been suffering from a groin injury, Baird was named amongst the substitutes for the play-off final:

"We won the game 1-0, thanks to a goal from Ronnie Mauge, and I'm not sure if it was Neil's way of getting back at me but he made me warm up all afternoon with no intention of putting me on.

"All that aside, it was a tremendous result for Plymouth Argyle and one of the many promotions on Neil Warnock's curriculum vitae. We had a fantastic journey back to Plymouth, and everybody was revelling in what we had achieved that season. The digs that Keith was staying in were above a public house, and we were in there celebrating for the whole of the next day before I made my way home to Hampshire."

Having being brought into Plymouth to do a specific job and the club achieving the target of promotion, Ian was looking forward to the new season:

"Pre-season was tough, but you expect that when Neil Warnock is your manager. I felt sharp and had played in a couple of friendlies in the centre of midfield, enjoying one particular game against Chelsea in which I had a good battle with Denis Wise.

"A couple of days later I scored in a win against Taunton Town. But then, out of the blue, Warnock informed me that Brighton & Hove Albion had come in for me. I had one year left on my contract but Warnock was willing to let me go.

"I had a good time at Plymouth, despite the ups and downs I had with Warnock. He is a strange character and everything that happened at the club revolved around him.

"When I was manager at Eastleigh, Warnock brought the team he was managing at the time to train down there, and the training and the routines were exactly the same as what he did when I played for him. Over the years his views on how the game should be played have never changed. He is very much set in his ways, but he has a certain charm that makes you want to play for him."

# 21

## The best and worst

The Liverpool legend Jimmy Case was the manager who signed Ian Baird for Brighton & Hove Albion – who at the time were in dire straits, beset with crippling off-the-field problems which threatened their very existence. Like his previous club Plymouth, The Seagulls were a side Ian had always seemed to do well against in the past:

"The Goldstone Ground had been a fairly lucky ground for me throughout my career, and I always looked at Brighton as a decent club. By the time I went there they had got themselves into a fair bit of mess off the field, and for most of the season it looked like we would be heading out of the Football League – which would have been a catastrophe."

Despite their well-documented problems, Brighton had been handing out decent contracts to the players they were bringing in, and Baird signed a two-year deal on £1,000 per week. Once again, Hayden was involved in overseeing the talks:

"Case was desperate to sign Bairdy, and the club broke the bank to ensure they secured his signature.

"Ian made a request to his new manager, and it was one I had never heard before or since. Bairdy knew that Case lived reasonably close to him in Southampton, and he asked him to pick him up each morning and drive him into training.

"To be fair to Case, he was fantastic with Ian. And once the negotiations were complete and the contract was signed and sealed, he took him out for a meal and they enjoyed a few beers. No manager had ever done that before in my experience."

Baird would enjoy his time playing under the former Liverpool hard man, but admits that it was not all plain sailing:

"He would join in the training sessions and it was easy to see that he'd been a top player. Jimmy had a horrendous reputation for boozing, yet he was a diamond and you'd struggle to meet a nicer bloke in football. His main downfall was that whilst he could be the best manager you could wish to have, he could also be the worst.

"On the first day I joined up for pre-season training, we were sent on a run up and down the hills and it would take about an hour. Jimmy told me that I could take my time and trot along at the back. I had other ideas. We were well into the run and Jimmy was waiting at the top of one of the hills, and I was about fourth or fifth from the front. He shouted to me that I shouldn't be there; I'd be ok at the back.

"I had always kept myself in good shape, and the last thing I wanted was for the other lads to think that I had joined the club to toss it off. That's what I mean about Jimmy's side of being the worst manager, he was far too nice.

"I never once saw him get angry, I never heard him raise his voice. He always wanted the best for the players, but some days at training he would ask us what we wanted to do. It shouldn't be like that. And due to the turmoil off the pitch and our poor form on it, the pressure began to take its toll. It would have been too much for any manager and it was certainly too much for Jimmy. You could smell the alcohol on him first thing in a morning. And he thought we could go out and play like Liverpool whereas in reality, we were a bunch of players collectively struggling at the foot of the Football League."

The season had started well for Brighton, with a 2-1 win over Chester City. It was also a good day for Ian who, on his debut, scored the equaliser in the 70th minute before George Parris netted the winner ten minutes later.

Baird also found the net in draws against Scunthorpe United and Torquay United. But even at that early stage of the season, the club's struggles were evident and they were sliding down the league table alarmingly. A home defeat to Lincoln City at the start of October prompted three separate pitch invasions, for which the club would eventually be docked two points by the Football League, and then a defeat in the following game – away at Wigan Athletic – saw Brighton rooted to the bottom of the table.

In truth, the football club was a rudderless ship, which was sailing towards the murky waters of non-league football. Between the 10th of September and the 29th of October, they picked up just two points from a possible 33.

On the 2nd of November, Albion travelled to Hartlepool, who occupied 23rd position in the league. It was the battle of the basement clubs and, despite falling behind in the ninth minute, Brighton fought back and claimed a much needed 3-2 win. Hartlepool were on an equally poor run, and this latest setback resulted in them sacking their manager Keith Houchen.

The FA Cup first round was played just two weeks later and, despite drawing non-league Sudbury Town, the competition failed to provide any respite for the beleaguered Jimmy Case. After drawing 0-0 in the first tie, Brighton fell behind in the replay at the Goldstone Ground. Although Craig Maskell equalised, the league's basement club was knocked out in a penalty shoot-out.

Baird was on the bench for the original fixture but was back in the side for the replay. He missed his spot kick in the shoot-out, which ended 4-3 to Sudbury.

Real pressure was mounting on Case – and with the cup exit coming in the middle of four straight league defeats, he was sacked on the 4th of December, with the club 11 points adrift at the bottom and heading into oblivion. Baird admits it was an extremely difficult time:

"As players we were lucky, because the battles in the boardroom were at the forefront of the supporters' minds. And they were too busy demonstrating about those issues to give us any real criticism.

"Some players were performing, but too many weren't and there was no camaraderie within the dressing room. The club had been in the FA Cup Final in 1983 and should have won it, and for this to happen just 13 years later was an absolute tragedy."

Due to no further involvement in the FA Cup, Brighton had a weekend off. By the time they took to the field on the 14th of December, Jimmy Case had been shown the door and a new manager was in charge:

"Steve Gritt was appointed along with his assistant Jeff Wood, and things began to change. My partnership up front with Craig Maskell started to click and the goals were flowing."

# 22

# The greatest of great escapes

Gritt's first game as manager of Brighton came against Hull City, and the new manager syndrome was evident as his side recorded a stunning 3-0 win. Stuart Storer scored the second Albion goal that day, and he acknowledged how things quickly changed under the new manager:

"It was far more professional under Steve Gritt. We worked hard and dug in to get the results. With Jimmy Case, training was too relaxed and that attitude rubbed off when we took to the field."

The New Year saw an incredible turnaround, with Brighton winning five consecutive home games as they battled to avoid the drop. Baird scored in victories over Rochdale, Hartlepool United, and Exeter City. He grabbed a brace in a win over Swansea City but he admitted the away form was a concern:

"We were superb at home – and after we lost against Darlington on the 3rd of December, we went the rest of the season unbeaten at the Goldstone Ground. However, we barely got anything on our travels, and that was something we needed to put right."

The club had been given a new lease of life, and Steve Gritt introduced teambuilding days in an attempt to improve the camaraderie and morale within the squad. He recalled an instance where the players spent the day on the golf course:

"Bairdy and Dave Martin had disappeared. Nobody knew where they had gone, until we returned to the hotel where we were staying on Brighton seafront. The pair of them were sat on the steps at the entrance to the building – eating burger and chips, absolutely pissed out of their minds."

Baird knew all about Dave Martin, having played with him at Bristol City, and he had a word with Steve Gritt about signing the midfielder who was then at Northampton Town:

"I advised Gritty to bring Dave to the club. He was a fantastic bloke to have in the dressing room and he could play a bit at that level. He was a good passer of the ball and a good organiser. His main problem was he was so slow – hence his nickname, 'The Diesel'.

"Dave signed on loan at the end of March – and the minute he walked into the dressing room, you would have thought he'd been there 20 years."

The pattern of winning at home and losing away more or less continued as the season reached its climax. The pressure was on but Brighton, despite being written off, remarkably, had safety in their sights.

On the 8th of March, Baird scored Brighton's third in an eight-goal thriller at home to Leyton Orient. The game ended all square, and it was the first time that the Seagulls had failed to win at the Goldstone since drawing with Colchester United on Boxing Day.

More goals were to come, first in a 2-0 win over Cardiff City and then a priceless 42nd minute winner at home to Barnet. But despite the scintillating home form, Gritt's side suffered five successive defeats on the road at Carlisle United, Darlington, Hull City, Chester City and Scunthorpe United before the sequence was broken with a 1-1 draw at Cambridge United.

It all made for an interesting final home game against Doncaster Rovers on the 26th of April – the day that would see Brighton & Hove Albion play at the Goldstone Ground, which had been their home since 1902, for the last time.

An emotional afternoon was in store. A wreath was laid on the top of the dug-out and the Last Post had been played. But come three o'clock, the three points were far more important than saying goodbye to the stadium.

Baird and the rest of the players knew that they had to beat Doncaster, who themselves needed a point to extinguish fears they might be the side that dropped into the non-league:

"It was an unbelievable occasion. We had played Mansfield Town earlier in the season in front of 1,933 fans, but for the Doncaster game over 11,000 turned up. We knew what we had to do and, due to our excellent home form and the fact the visitors hadn't had the best of seasons either, we were confident."

The game sparked into life after 18 minutes, as Baird battled for the ball with Doncaster's giant centre back Darren Moore. The pair became embroiled in a tangle, followed by a punch-up in which several other players from both sides became involved. The referee had little option but to show Moore and Baird red cards, and the latter concedes he was lucky:

"It wasn't the greatest idea I've ever had in my life. Darren is a monster of a man and I was very lucky he didn't fill me in as we walked down the tunnel."

Steve Gritt admits that although losing Baird was a huge blow, Doncaster came off worse with the loss of their colossal central defender:

"Looking back it affected them more than it did us. Both sides were down to ten men and I thought we could still go on and win the game. Saying that, God only knows what went through Ian's mind. Only he could get involved in a fight with a man the size of Darren Moore."

Brighton's closest rivals in the battle to survive, Hereford United, were away at Leyton Orient. Albion knew that if they beat Doncaster and Hereford lost, they would travel to Hereford's Edgar Street ground on the final day of the season. There, they would need a point if they were to stay up and pull off the greatest of great escapes.

Both games were 0-0 at half-time, but spirits at the Goldstone Ground were lifted as news filtered through that Leyton Orient had taken the lead at Brisbane Road in the 54th minute. Ten minutes later, Orient extended their advantage before bedlam at Brighton.

In the 67th minute Albion attacked and, after a Mark Morris header hit the Doncaster cross-bar, Stuart Storer gleefully volleyed in the rebound from close range. It would prove to be the decisive goal on an unbelievable afternoon, which was made all the better by Leyton Orient's 2-1 win over Hereford. Brighton were off the bottom of the league for the first time since October, knowing their destiny was in their own hands. Steve Gritt, speaking at the time, was confident that his side held the advantage despite their abysmal away form:

"Now we've actually got ourselves off the bottom of the league, I think the psychological boost of that – I hope – will certainly be a boost for us and probably be a bit of a downer for Hereford now. You know, they've had so long above us and we've had so long to get off the bottom. And now we're there, I know the players won't want to go back down there again."

It all made for another tense week for everybody connected with Brighton & Hove Albion. Baird remembers the celebrity Albion fans having their say:

"Des Lynam was on the radio and television, stressing how important it was that we got the required point against Hereford. He said what we all knew: it would be a tragedy if the club found itself in the non-league when the full-time whistle was blown at Edgar Street.

"I was in the hotel the night before, and I had stressed to 'The Diesel' that it would be a disaster if this crop of players – of which we were involved – were the ones responsible for a club like Brighton & Hove Albion dropping out of the Football League. The consequences were frightening."

Brighton took a few thousand fans to Hereford, and many more travelled without tickets for a game which they could ill afford to lose. The match was played on a bumpy pitch on a windy day and it was the home side who struck first. Hereford took the lead after 21 minutes, when Tony Agana hammered a shot across the goalmouth that Kerry Mayo inadvertently turned into his own net.

It wasn't until the 62nd minute that Brighton equalised. Craig Maskell's shot was pushed onto the post by the Hereford goalkeeper, but Seagulls substitute Robbie Reinelt was on hand to capitalise on the rebound. The goal, arguably the most important in the club's long history, sent the travelling fans into raptures.

As the clock ticked down, Brighton knew they would be safe with a point despite Maskell and Baird squandering opportunities to win the game.

The full-time whistle was blown and the travelling Brighton fans were delirious. Robbie Reinelt, a £15,000 signing from Colchester United just a few months before, had become a Brighton legend with one single kick of a football. Steve Gritt's side had achieved the unachievable and escaped relegation, having at one time been 14 points adrift at the foot of the table. It was a moment to savour and one that Baird and his team-mates enjoyed:

"There was a relief that we had stayed up, and there was a relief that a traumatic season had come to an end with the right outcome as far as we were concerned. You can imagine the celebrations on the way home that evening.

"I remember in the aftermath of it all, Gritty arranged a night out for the players and staff. We had a meal and enjoyed several beers – before out of the blue, later on in the night, Jimmy Case turned up and made a speech, wearing his slippers. He was pissed out of his brains.

"No other ex-manager would have done that, but that was Jimmy. He had been put in an invidious situation, but looking back he played a part in Brighton & Hove Albion staying up. Although Gritty and Jeff Wood deserve the credit, as they made us fitter and sharper to get the results which proved decisive in the end, a lot of us had been brought to the club by Jimmy Case.

"I departed Brighton the following season. The club was looking to make cuts, and my contract was terminated by mutual consent. After a long career I was facing up to life without football, and I was at a crossroads in my life."

Baird owned a wine bar named *Willy's*, but admits it was never going to earn him a fortune. Like many players leaving the game, he panicked a little and frantically sought ways of staying in football and continuing to earn a living.

"I approached 'Duke Box' (Ian Juryeff), who I was an apprentice with when it all began at Southampton. He was back at Saints, and responsible for the community work. I saw this as a possible route into coaching."

Ian was already making strides in obtaining his FA coaching licence, but was halted by the transition as the FA licence was scrapped to move in line with UEFA:

"Ian Juryeff was brilliant for me. He gave me three sessions per week visiting the local schools, advising the youngsters. I envisaged this as being the first steps and I welcomed the experience."

# 23

# Sid James with a hangover!

Opportunities were offered to Ian to continue playing. Geoff Butler, manager of Salisbury City, persuaded Ian to turn out for the Southern Premier League outfit. He made his debut on the 20th of December 1997, in front of just 221 supporters. Despite not scoring, Ian played his part in a 4-0 win against Sittingbourne.

He left the club after making just three appearances. His last was on New Year's Day 1998:

"I had been offered £350 per week to become Geoff's assistant manager at Salisbury. However Mick Leonard, the ex-Notts County goalkeeper, had been very persistent in trying to get me over to Hong Kong. He was out there playing for a side called Instant Dict, who were named after the firm who owned them. The company manufactured pocket computerised dictionaries which also acted as translating devices.

"I knew that I would have to go out there on an initial month's trial. That's how it worked and I had told Mick that, if they gave me a grand a week for the month, I would go to Hong Kong."

Despite struggling with a knee problem (which he kept to himself) and not having a clue what to expect, Ian realised that the opportunity was too good to turn down and was intent on giving it a go:

"I'd turned out for Salisbury City on Boxing Day, in a game which was played in atrocious weather conditions. Hailstones the size of golf balls were coming down and it was freezing cold. I wasn't getting any younger, and at that stage of my career the move to Asia had to be the better option."

A day after playing his final game for Salisbury City, Baird travelled to Hong Kong on the 2nd of January 1998, flying into Kai Tak Airport. He was met by a barrage of reporters, photographers and club officials – and Mick Leonard, who recalls the circumstances leading up to the striker's arrival:

"Despite Instant Dict having a fairly decent side, a director – Ken Ng – told me that he thought the club needed a striker. He asked if I could get him a centre-forward who was big, strong and could find the back of the net. I laughed and told him it was highly unlikely. But I could maybe get him a lad called Ian Baird.

"After speaking to Bairdy many times, he eventually agreed to come over and it was big news. The press were waiting for him at the airport, and as he came walking through Arrivals I pointed him out to Ken, who turned to me with a puzzled look on his face and asked, 'Who the fuck is this?'

"To be fair to Ken, Bairdy looked dishevelled to say the least. He resembled Sid James with a hangover."

During the many conversations that Baird had with Mick Leonard, nothing prepared him for what he encountered on his arrival:

"Mick and Ken took me out for a meal and told me all about the place, the way of life and the football club. It was all a bit of a blur – I was jet-lagged and somewhat confused. We then arrived at a hotel on Discovery Bay, which is on the south-eastern coast of Lantau Island. That is where I would be residing during my stay.

"Lantau Island is the largest island in Hong Kong and is situated at the mouth of the Pearl River. It was like living in a fantasy world, the place is absolutely unbelievable. There were no cars; people used buses and golf carts as their means of transport."

At the time that Baird arrived, the domestic football season had closed for almost two weeks due to the annual Carlsberg Tournament taking place. He trained alone, knowing that his month's trial had been reduced to just over a fortnight:

"Before I could play a competitive game in Hong Kong I had to pass a Cooper test, in which I had to complete at least eight laps of a 400-metre track in no more than 12 minutes. I had to train hard. It was by no means easy to complete the challenge, especially with a dodgy knee.

"Thankfully I passed the test, received my permission to play and I got down to business scoring a bag full of goals in the first few games that I played in

– including a hat-trick in a 6-1 win over a team called Rangers. And it was agreed that I would stay on until the end of that season.

"The biggest thing for me – and this is no disrespect to the players involved – but I couldn't believe the amounts of money they were earning and I wanted a slice of it. It was easy street compared to playing in England.

"There were many British lads out there playing in the league for various clubs. But in rather incestuous fashion, they all stuck together and lived on Discovery Bay. They included Tim O'Shea, a former Gillingham defender who was at Instant Dict, whilst my old Portsmouth team-mate Martin Kuhl was at Happy Valley, along with Peter Guthrie the former Barnet goalkeeper. Ex-Aston Villa defender Shaun Teale was playing for Sing Tao. In addition Ian Muir, the former Tranmere Rovers striker, was also in Hong Kong."

# 24

# Turmoil in Paradise

By the end of the season Instant Dict had won the League and FA Cup double, and Ian was offered an 18-month contract on £1700 per week,

"It was staggering. I had gone from facing an uncertain future, pondering a £350 per week offer from Salisbury, to be earning easy money and living in paradise with a knee that was in bits.

"It was an outdoor lifestyle, and there was many a drunken night sitting out on the plaza. The social life was superb and I felt like the luckiest man alive."

Mick Leonard, the man largely responsible for Ian's unbelievable change of fortune, remembers all too well some memorable incidents on nights out:

"One night we decided to take a trip to Peng Chau, which is a small island off the north-eastern coast of Lantau island. The journey takes around ten minutes by ferry.

"We knew that the last return ferry left at 10:50pm but, after a gallon of Stella and a bottle of red wine, we missed it and had to pay one of the locals £25 to take us back in his own boat.

"We were stood in complete darkness on the jetty, rather worse for wear. I was standing some distance away from Bairdy, and I turned around to find he had disappeared. It became evident that he had stepped off the jetty and fallen 20 foot into the sea. He managed to swim back to the steps and climb back up, before we had a huge argument when he accused me of pushing him into the water.

"On another occasion, straight after a game, we had gone to a bar named *'Dusk till Dawn'* for a few pints. We soon noticed that Roger Lloyd Pack, the guy who played the part of Trigger in *Only Fools and Horses*, was in the establishment minding his own business.

"Bairdy kept looking over at Roger and smiling to himself, and I knew he was going to say something. Eventually, he walked over to the actor and said, 'Alright Trig? Can you say it, go on say it, just the once'. You could see that Roger wasn't impressed. He glared at Bairdy and replied in his characters voice, 'Alright Dave... now fuck off'."

The next step for Baird was to get Lesley, Amy and Liam to join him. And, despite Lesley's original doubts the family were over in Hong Kong by the start of the following season:

"We found ourselves a lovely apartment and put the kids into school. Amy and Liam loved it out there, it was a safe society and the type of environment where you didn't have to worry about them when they were not with you. Also, the experience brought Liam out of his shell."

When the new campaign got underway, Instant Dict – nicknamed the Dickies – drew their opening game 2-2 with South China. But when it was discovered that the Dickies had fielded a suspended player, the league awarded South China the points with a 3-0 score line:

"We didn't get off to the best of starts. And before I knew where I was, Ken Ng had offered me the role as first team coach in place of Khoo Luam Khen, who I always thought he wasn't particularly keen on. Khoo stayed with me on the coaching staff, but it put me in a predicament with the lads who had been my team-mates and all of a sudden I was their manager.

"We lost the FA Cup Final on golden goal, which was hugely disappointing. The Chinese do not accept defeat, and they are not prepared to sit and listen to any sort of excuse.

"It was a great experience being first team coach, and it stood me in good stead for when I was asked to manage the national side. I took charge for three Asia Cup qualifying games against Indonesia, Thailand and Singapore. We failed to qualify, but the opportunity I was presented with enabled me to understand the politics of Asian football and it capped off a whirlwind start to life in Hong Kong."

The role was all new to Baird, and he openly admits that he made a couple of fatal mistakes. One of them was the signing of a player from a club called Happy Valley, which in the end brought disastrous consequences:

"The lad in question had been a very average player over in England, but possessed the right attributes to be a success in the Hong Kong league. Mainly that he stood 6 foot 4.

"He had played for Happy Valley the season before, and had scored his fair share of goals. I thought he was technically good and could finish, but Ken Ng wasn't keen. In the end, I persuaded Ken to sign him and I knew my arse was on the line.

"We travelled to Singapore as part of our preparations for the new season, and I instantly knew that I had made a mistake. It turned out that he wasn't as good as I thought he was, and also he didn't have the work ethic that I deemed necessary. The lad had put me under pressure straight away. He didn't play very well in Singapore, and in one game I had to take him off before he was sent off for a scything challenge that is far from appreciated over there.

"However, the biggest mistake I made with him was when I asked Lesley to keep her eye on him. He was a young lad who liked a drink, and in the past had gone off the rails. I wanted Lesley to ensure he was eating the right food and looking after himself, and she was very receptive to the idea.

"In the meantime the side was struggling and, following a 2-1 defeat to Sai Kung, we were languishing just three places off the bottom of the league table. We had won just two of the first eight games and had also lost in the Senior Shield semi-finals.

"Ken called me to a meeting in his favourite hotel. And over a buffet breakfast, he told me that he had made the hardest decision of his life and I had been sacked as first team coach at Instant Dict. He then informed me that my contract would be paid in full, and he asked me to sit around and do nothing but live off the money for three to four months – as he was buying another football club and he wanted me to manage them. There was no way I was going to do nothing and, when I heard that Happy Valley wanted to sign me, I didn't hesitate to go and play for them.

"I had no choice. But once Ken discovered I had joined Happy Valley, he cut me off like I had never existed – but that was the least of my worries in all honesty.

"I endured a nightmare time at Happy Valley, I didn't enjoy it one bit, and I began to get the feeling that my marriage to Lesley was going wrong. She had everything she could have wished for, but she was always moaning and telling me that she wasn't happy.

"I went away with my new club for a tournament in Brunei. Clubs from all over the Far East were taking part, and we knew that we could be there for 10 days or three weeks – depending how far we progressed.

"Alcohol consumption is forbidden in Brunei, and it turned out to be the most depressing trip I had ever been on. It was worse than going to Sweden with Portsmouth, at least there was lager in Sweden.

"We got through to the final, but there was absolutely nothing to do in between the football and the training. After winning the semi-final, we had to wait four days before the final was played – and the directors, realising the boredom had set in, took us on a trip to Penang.

"That was more like it. Pete Guthrie and I spent the whole time on the piss. But whilst I had been away, Lesley had not been answering any of my calls and I knew something was seriously wrong.

"Just after I returned from Brunei, my brothers Darren, Gavin, their partners and a couple of mates came over to stay with us. And it was then that I discovered that Lesley and the young player I had asked her to keep her eye on had been having an affair. I was shattered when I found out, and I did what any man would do. I beat the fuck out of him. I went over to his apartment – and although he knew that I had discovered what had been going on, he let me in. We had a good old scrap, but I started to get the better of him and tried to smash a television over his head. Then, all of a sudden, Lesley turned up and tried to pull me off him.

"I was in a bad place. I avoided training due to the fact that I was in pieces, and I knew I had to get back to England before the situation got any worse. I booked a flight and that was the end of my time in 'paradise'."

# 25

# Wrongful dismissal

Following the abrupt end to life in Hong Kong, Ian spent a full week trying to find the answer to his problems at the bottom of a bottle:

"I was practically living in the pub. I could not believe what had happened and I was well and truly devastated. After a week my Dad came to find me, and told me I needed to sort myself out as I still had Amy and Liam to think about and I needed to get my kids back to England.

"I adored Lesley and had given her all she could ever want. I had come from a broken home and that is the last thing I ever wanted for my kids. I can never truly forgive her for what she did."

Ian paid for his wife and children to return home. But just a fortnight later, he was back on a flight to Hong Kong:

"Hong Kong was the last place on Earth that I wanted to be. I knew a lot of people, and they were all aware of the circumstances in which I had left just weeks earlier. But I had a long-term commitment to play in a veteran's tournament over there. I boarded the plane with Gordon Strachan, Paul Davis and Jimmy Quinn, and I was in a complete daze. I remember thinking during the flight that I wouldn't care less if the plane went down. It was going to be tough facing all those people, but I couldn't let the organisers of the tournament down.

"Every night I would go out on the piss and not get to my bed until six o'clock the following morning – but due to the frame of mind I was in, I could not get drunk no matter how hard I tried. But even so, it was a miracle that I found the mental and physical strength to play in those games."

On his return to Hampshire, Ian knew he had a lot to sort out and he needed to find employment. Eventually he got himself involved with a company called

RMR, who were website developers and also specialised in on-line conferencing.

Businessman Jason Hill had dealings with RMR. He, along with Baird, invested in the company and helped raised sufficient funds to enable them to float on the stock market:

"In April 2000, RMR floated on the AIM market for a significant amount, and we were very happy people. But it didn't last too long. In no time at all shares fell to 5p, not helped by the collapse of the NASDAQ, and I left the company in 2002."

Despite initially being kept busy in his role with RMR, Ian was still struggling. He had many sleepless nights and was finding it hard to function. He was undertaking an unfamiliar role as office manager, but another opportunity in football was not too far away:

"Tim O'Shea had returned to England, and had gone to Farnborough. He repeatedly asked me if I fancied turning out for them although I had no idea what league Farnborough played in. I delayed my decision, but eventually agreed to go down there, give it a go and see what developed.

"It transpired they were playing in the Ryman Premier League, and were managed by Graham Westley. My first impressions of Westley, who had purchased a controlling interest at the football club and appointed himself as manager, were not good. I thought he was a bit off the wall."

Despite Ian's fitness levels being far away from what was required, he played one pre-season friendly and felt he did alright. He was offered a deal by Westley, which took him by surprise:

"The deal on the table was £200 per week, and it would be a 10-game trial. I was gobsmacked. I knew some of the other lads were earning double that, and had been given cars and other perks.

"There were some real good lads at the club, including Jimmy Dack, Steve Watson, Barry Laker and Justin Gregory. They could play as well – I was very impressed with the standard. I decided to get my head down, improve my fitness levels and get through the trial although it was a frustrating time.

"I came on as substitute in consecutive games and scored in both, before being handed a start against Purfleet. We won that game 2-0, yet I was back on the bench for the following fixture. It was annoying, but the team was winning and it was Westley's job to make the decisions."

In a team meeting just before Christmas, Ian told a few people some home truths and unfortunately it did him no favours. He was dropped from the squad for games against Slough Town and Aldershot, which was a big derby game at that level.

Meanwhile on a personal front, Ian and Lesley were attempting to patch things up. But despite enjoying a nice family Christmas, Baird realised he was fighting a lost cause:

"We had a lovely time celebrating the festive period, but things were never quite the same. Lesley told me she wanted to go out and earn some money, and got herself a job working behind the bar in the local pub.

"Unbelievably she started another affair, and that was the end of our marriage. The experience left me very bitter. In my time as a professional footballer we earned a fraction of what the players earn today – but when I started out at Southampton, I set myself a target to be mortgage-free at the age of 35 with money in the bank.

"By the time the divorce came through, I was 37 years old. I owed just £25,000 on a £600,000 property and had a tidy sum in savings, which soon went out of the window.

"As soon as Lesley received her divorce settlement cheque, she immediately bought her new boyfriend a new car – a Jaguar which cost £32,000 of my money. It topped off a sickening experience for me and proved to be a very bitter pill to swallow."

As the season entered the New Year, Farnborough were flying. They won 14 out of 15 games between the 27th of January and the 9th of April. However, that game on the 9th of April brought an end to Baird's season:

"We played away at Hendon and, due to the conditions that evening, Graham Westley wanted the referee to call the game off. He didn't, and the match went ahead.

"I played centre midfield that night, and during the first half I received the ball, controlled it and laid it off. As I turned, a Hendon player came straight through me and took my standing leg. The pain was incredible and I had to be carried off and taken to the local hospital, accompanied by Jimmy Dack and the club physio. The place was a shithole, and the queues to get into Accident and Emergency were like the January sales."

Ian's patience ran out. He decided to leave the hospital and they drove to Southampton General:

"I was in shock, and the pain had become unbearable. They rushed me straight in, and I was diagnosed with a broken tibia, broken fibula, my ankle ligaments were ruptured and the ankle itself was dislocated. The doctors immediately gave me gas and air, and repaired the dislocation before potting the leg."

Graham Westley had instructed Ian not to let the medical team at Southampton General treat him. He arranged for Bairdy to undergo the necessary operation in a private hospital in Wimbledon:

"I spent the next 10 days in there. It was a fantastic but totally unexpected gesture from Westley. In addition, he came to visit me and offered me a new one-year deal on increased money, which provided me some security in an otherwise uncertain period of my life."

An 18-year playing career, which had started on Saturday the 19th of February 1983 in the English First Division, had ended with a sickening injury suffered in front of 684 people at Hendon in the Ryman Premier League.

Farnborough finished the season as league champions, and were promoted to the Conference. As a reward, the club took the playing staff and management on a golfing holiday to Portugal. Due to Ian's injury he was unable to get his clubs out, along with Tim O'Shea and Darren Annon, whose injuries also prevented them from participating:

"We couldn't play golf and we were abroad in the sunshine, so what else was there to do? We hit the booze for four days, we were absolutely flat out on the piss. As a result, we became the hotel nuisances and upset a few people with our antics.

"On the last night I'd lost my crutches in a night club, and the following morning I went down for breakfast in a wheelchair. I could sense there was a problem and the club captain, Steve Watson, approached me to advise Westley had gone mental due to somebody faking his signature and paying a bar bill."

The fingers were pointed at Baird, O'Shea and Annon. Ian admitted to signing a couple of bar bills, but they were in his own signature. Despite pleading his innocence the issue didn't go away.

"I found out who the culprit was and he had little intention of owning up. I advised him that if I took the blame, he would have to cover any fine I was given. Once back in England, Westley called us all to a hotel for a meeting to discuss the incident. The lads were sat there, and in turn the manager said his piece to each and every one of them. He turned to me and informed me I had been brilliant to have around the place, but he was sacking me for signing the bar bill."

# 26

# HN Asia and the end of IBMH

Ian had first met Hayden Evans, the managing director of West Yorkshire-based HN Sports, during his second spell at Leeds United. After overhearing a conversation Baird was having with Noel Blake about Test Match cricket, Hayden arranged to obtain Ian some tickets.

The friendship built from there, and developed into a working relationship when – accepting that the injury suffered at Hendon had called time on his long career on the playing field – Baird tried his hand in the player's agency business and went to work for HN Sports:

"I was working with other ex-players – including the likes of the ex-Leeds centre-forward Imre Varadi, my old team mate John Pearson, and Peter Jackson, whose clubs included Bradford City, Newcastle United and Huddersfield Town.

"All was well and I built up a nice portfolio of business. Partnerships had been struck with Scott Fisher, who identified the best young talent in Scotland, and my old mate Eammon Collins, who did the same over in the Republic of Ireland – where I would spend one week every month.

"On the books we had the likes of Alan McGregor, Charlie Adam, Scott Brown, Kevin Thompson, Steven Fletcher, Glenn Whelan, Stephen Ireland, Willo Flood, Noel Hunt and Kevin Doyle. The whole experience was proving quite enjoyable.

"I knew I had to chase my tail and earn as much money as I could. Totalling up the divorce, it had cost me the best part of £400,000. And I had invested £75,000 in RMR, which didn't go particularly well."

Whilst over in Dublin, Ian would speak to the parents of young players who were hoping to fashion themselves a career in football. He would have as many as ten meetings a day, in a bid to tie up deals and get promising young-sters on the books. Even then, there was no real guarantee that they would make the grade in professional football; even if they did, the rules stated that they could only sign a two-year deal with the agency:

"You have to play a waiting game in the agency business. A lot of money is laid out on travelling, accommodation and entertainment but the finan-cial rewards are not instant. And although I was under the umbrella of HN Sports, Hayden was not getting paid either. It was all about future earnings.

"An opportunity then arose to expand into Asia. Big money was being offered to get players over to China. It wasn't an easy nut to crack however, and the first sticking point was that I needed a Chinese business partner."

Through contacts, Ian was introduced to Tony Xue. Then he found an investor to offset the costs in his friend Dino Zavagno, who was involved in Financial Services in Hong Kong:

"Dino saw this as a decent business venture, and he was prepared to put a significant amount of money into it. I based myself in China and had several meetings with Tony Xue. And after gaining his trust, he affiliated himself to HN Sports and we set up HN Asia."

Ian spent 18 months travelling around China with Tony, and it proved to be a fantastic experience. But frustrations soon grew:

"Tony knew some very influential people all over China, and we did little deals here and little deals there. But then I started getting annoyed.

"We were trying to bring players in, but things just weren't happening. There were opportunities to take David May and Ramon Vega over there. But the Chinese clubs wanted them to go on trial, something the players weren't prepared to do, and as the money was starting to dry up I desper-ately needed something to happen.

"We set up a deal for the Colombian and ex-Middlesbrough strik-er Hamilton Ricard to sign for Shenzhen. The deal would see us earn 250,000USD, and that money would have enabled us to continue running HN Asia for a further year.

"However, nothing was straightforward. Like May and Vega, they requested that Ricard came over on trial, which he refused. The Chinese then changed their minds – they decided that a trial wasn't necessary, and the deal looked like it was back on.

"Ricard needed to obtain a Chinese Visa, which took five days. But then he advised that he was only coming if he could bring his mother, his brother and his two kids. We agreed to his demands, but then had another five-day wait whilst those members of his family acquired their own Visas.

"Further demands were made when he insisted that they fly First Class, and after some haggling he got his wish. The flights were booked – and in order for us to receive our payment, all Ricard had to do was turn up at Shenzhen, play one game and put in a half decent performance.

"We had a colleague waiting at Bogota airport over in Colombia, to ensure that Ricard got on the flight. But due to the number of days spent waiting for all the Visas to be issued, our man had outstayed his welcome and his own Visa had expired. He had to leave, and it was now a case of trusting Ricard to arrive at the airport and board the flight to China.

"That 'Baird bad luck' then struck again. Hamilton Ricard checked in at the airport, but our deal was hijacked when some other club offered him more money than we had."

It proved to be the end of HN Asia and Baird, with his tail between his legs, came back to the United Kingdom:

"The money had run out and, due to the collapse of the Ricard deal, I had lost all credibility with Tony Xue. I had little option but to return to England, and the Chinese adventure had come to a sticky end."

Once back in England, Ian was able to give full attention to his business IBMH (Ian Baird Motor Holdings), which was a vehicle sales/leasing company that Ian had formed with his business partner Russell Vaughan. Initially, it was one that proved to be a real success.

Russell, who has been involved with Ian over a number of business ventures, admits that at first it was tough working with Baird due to his footballing background:

"Not once did Ian play on the fact that he had been a professional footballer, but customers and corporate partners would. It could get quite awkward and difficult in business meetings. We would be round a table and I would ask a question to the person we were negotiating a contract with, and they would provide their response but look straight at Ian whilst they were talking.

"It was pretty uncomfortable for both of us at times. But I suppose, in the long run, his name helped us and the business was quite a success.

"It could be a laugh a minute with Bairdy. There was one occasion when I was on the forecourt showing a customer our range of motors and was trying to do the deal. I heard a commotion – Bairdy was having an argument with an employee. Then in full view of the customer, Bairdy was knocking ten bells of shit out of the lad that worked for us."

Business was good. IBMH were importing cars from Germany, and an employee who helped look after the administrative side was placing advertisements in the Sunday Times. But after returning from a holiday, Ian realised that something didn't seem quite right:

"I was doing some book work, and alarm bells immediately started ringing. Deposits were going missing, and it transpired that an employee had done several deals to sell cars to a group of very colourful characters.

"Things came to a head when one morning some geezer was sitting in our offices, expecting his brand new Bentley to be waiting for him on our forecourt. In an attempt to defuse the situation, I let him drive away in my BMW 6 series – which thankfully I got back, but at a cost.

"In the end we were sat in the offices of the guys that had made all the deposits, and to bring the whole experience to an end we had to return their cash. We parted with £30,000 and walked away, closing IBMH in the process."

# 27

# Football management and a gentleman's agreement

In 2003, soon after Farnborough had lost 5-1 to Arsenal in a FA Cup tie, Graham Westley resigned as manager and withdrew his financial backing. He was then appointed manager of Stevenage, who were struggling at the bottom end of the Conference, and – in a strange twist – he turned to Ian Baird:

"I received a phone call one day, and it was Graham Westley asking me to meet him at a hotel in Richmond. Having not spoken to him since the day he fired me over the bar bill incident, I was surprised to say the least."

To Baird's amazement, Westley admitted he had got things wrong over the incident at Farnborough, and he offered Ian the job as his assistant at Stevenage. Ian acknowledged that the offer was decent and, although the club was struggling in the league, he knew that under Westley they had a chance:

"His style was unique and his training methods were different. But he had a burning desire, and although I knew he would apply a winning mentality within the club, I wasn't sure about accepting the role. In total I was offered the job on three occasions. Stevenage even announced on their official website that I had agreed to take the role, but I turned it down. I decided it wasn't the right move for me at that time."

Despite rejecting the chance offered by Westley, Ian wanted to return to football in a coaching capacity. He wouldn't have too long to wait.

In January 2004, Havant & Waterlooville were struggling – and Liam Daish and Mick Jenkins, who were joint managers, had been dismissed. Baird knew Peter Demott, one of the Havant directors, and he was interviewed for the job.

Originally Ian was unsuccessful, and the position was given to Dave Leworthy. However, the club continued to struggle, and Leworthy would only be in the job until November.

Simon Lynch worked as the Havant & Waterlooville match day programme editor at the time, and he admitted that the club was in a gradual decline under Dave Leworthy. There was a lack of discipline, with some of the players disrespecting the manager – and on occasions it was difficult to pinpoint who was actually in charge.

Within a week of Leworthy's sacking, Ian got the call. He was appointed as manager of the Hawks, who were playing in the Conference South, with Shaun Gale as his assistant:

"I could not have had a better assistant than Shaun Gale, he was fantastic. Also I had Adi Aymes, the former cricketer, as part of my backroom staff. Adi was the fitness coach and had been a half decent footballer in his youth."

Baird's reign could not have got off to a worse start, when Havant travelled to Weymouth for the first game of his tenure on the 4th of December 2004. It was a rude awakening to life in the managerial hot seat, as within 30 minutes his new side were 3-0 down. Ian made three changes at half-time and, after some strong words, he witnessed a courageous fight-back in the second half. But the game ended in a 3-2 defeat and it was not the start that Ian had been hoping for:

"Weymouth had been the big spenders in the division and had a huge wage bill. We were shocking in the first half, and I knew at that point that we had lots of hard work in front of us to turn things round."

The next game was just two days away, a home clash with Basingstoke Town. Baird demanded an improvement; he made several changes to his starting line-up and the team responded, thumping the visitors 5-1 with ex-Wimbledon striker Dean Holdsworth among the goals. It gave the club their first league win in almost two months.

The fixture marked a return to Havant & Waterlooville for Shaun Wilkinson, who had previously left the club to join Weymouth. Baird signed Wilkinson on loan, and his impressive performance went some way to repairing his strained relationship with the fans. It wasn't the first time that the pair had crossed paths, as Shaun pointed out:

"I had signed a professional contract at Brighton & Hove Albion some years before, and Micky Adams the manager advised me to get an agent. He put me in touch with Bairdy and John Pearson, who were working for HN Sports, and they began to look after my interests."

Like all new managers, Baird wanted to stamp his authority on the club and do things his way. There was a major turnover of players, and he managed to get rid of a few who he classed as 'wrong uns':

"When I arrived at the club I saw what state it was in, and there were players who should have been taken to court for impersonating footballers. I changed a few things and brought in some fresh faces, including the ex-Wimbledon player Peter Fear and Jamie Mackie, to replace the ones I didn't want. And although I had inherited some great lads such as Gareth Howells, Dean Holdsworth, and Joe Jordan's son Tom, it took a while for results to improve despite Holdsworth's goals.

"When things did improve, we won two successive home games and we went on a decent run, avoiding relegation quite comfortably. Dean Holdsworth was phenomenal and there is no doubt that, without his influence and goals, we would have gone down."

Expectations remained low at the start of the following season. But after a sticky start, things improved – despite the loss of Holdsworth, who joined Derby County as assistant manager to Phil Brown.

Rocky Baptiste was brought in. He played a major part in a season which would have seen Havant reach the play-offs, if it hadn't been for a decision made by the Football Conference:

"I had signed Tony Taggart from Weymouth just before Christmas, and there was a gentleman's agreement between the two clubs that he wouldn't play when we met Weymouth at the start of January.

"However, I had three players struggling with food poisoning and I had no option but to play Taggart in what was a massive game."

Ian approached the Chairman and the club secretary Trevor Brock, and asked what the worst outcome would be. He was informed that there was the risk of a fine if the visitors objected to Taggart's inclusion.

It would prove to be a controversial day. In a game which saw the Hawks win 2-1 and move to the top of the league, Weymouth alleged that a ball-boy took a throw-in which led to one of Havant's goals. Weymouth also made a complaint about the inclusion of Tony Taggart. In Baird's view, Havant got a rough deal:

"We had to attend a hearing, from which the panel decided that we should be docked three points for fielding an ineligible player. Mel Stein represented us at the case, but I feel that the committee were influenced by Weymouth as they had been the division's big spenders.

"The original decision was to replay the game without Taggart's involvement. It was a decision we appealed – but at the appeal hearing, we learnt that we would be docked three points and fined £1,000. The points deduction cost us a place in the end-of-season play-offs, which was obviously a massive blow."

Baird was confident that Havant could go one better during the next campaign. And, with Dean Holdsworth returning to the club after his departure from Derby County, he was happy with his squad.

Havant lost two of the first three games of the 2006-07 season. But things quickly picked up. With the prolific Baptiste scoring for fun it was no surprise that, despite a late stumble, the Hawks qualified for the play-offs – where they would play Braintree Town.

Braintree had finished third, just one point above Havant in fourth place, and there was very little to choose between the two sides. Both league fixtures had finished all square, with the game at Westleigh Park being a particularly spicy encounter.

The game descended into a farce after frustrations boiled over. In the first half the referee halted the game to speak to both managers after the visitors claimed that Rocky Baptiste had floored one of their players, Ollie Adejadi, with a punch.

The referee, Richard Martin, was losing control. He had sent Adi Aymes to the stands, and he was stopping the game at every opportunity which resulted in six minutes of injury time at the end of a first half.

In the second half, Baird followed Aymes after an incident with Braintree's Louis Riddle, who had broken clear down the wing. Baird threw a ball at him from the sidelines which Riddle angrily kicked back in Baird's direction. Both received red cards, along with the opposition's notorious manager George Borg.

The first leg of the play-offs would be at Havant's Westleigh Park ground. Baird wanted his players to concentrate on the game to follow, not the previous meeting:

"It was a massive game at a crucial time. Obviously the play-offs are heart-breaking occasions for the losers, and we had to make sure we were focused on being the team that were successful in gaining promotion."

It wasn't to be. A late goal from substitute Jefferson Louis ensured a 1-1 draw in the first leg – and another late goal at Braintree's Cressing Road, a Jamie Collins penalty, ensured the sides were level on aggregate. Unfortunately after extra time, Havant lost out in a penalty shootout and the promotion dream was over.

Ian, along with everybody connected with the club, was obviously devastated that they had come so near yet so far. But Simon Lynch recognised that Baird, although very upset, remained dignified.

In preparation for the new season, the squad spent some time in Wales. It was a trip that Matt Gray will always remember:

"I had just been appointed as Bairdy's assistant manager. But I was at a cross-roads with regards to whether I should go on a night out with the lads, as I had always done, or should I go with the staff and directors.

"I decided that it was only right that I join up with the staff at a curry house although I'm not a fan of curries. There were 12 of us at the table, a ton of food had been demolished, the drink was flowing and I'd had four pints of lager with not a bite to eat.

"When the bill came, Bairdy decided that we should play spoof and the eventual loser would foot the bill. Bearing in mind I had only drank four pints and the bill was £800, I was reluctant to join in but I had to bow to the pressure and participate.

"It reached the stage where there were seven of us left in. I called it right and I was out. In congratulating me, a colleague leant across the table and shook my hand. Bairdy immediately jumped on this and informed us that under the rules, no celebrations were allowed. And he insisted that I was reinstated into the game.

"Eventually, there were two people left, it was the 'final' and it was me up against Bairdy to determine who paid the bill. Bairdy called it right with five. I could not believe it, I felt sick. Four pints had cost me £800.

"I walked upstairs to go to the toilet. Bairdy followed me up and opened the door about an inch. He whispered, 'Daddy, Daddy, can you help me? I'm in

Wales and I've got myself involved in some big boys' shit. I need you to help me.'

"Bairdy was revelling in it, he really started to take the piss. I wandered back downstairs and approached the waiter to ask for the bill. I knew I would have to take it on the chin and put it down to experience. Bairdy advised me to check the bill with the Directors before paying it. I went over to the table to find they had chipped in and settled the bill, leaving me a very relieved man."

The summer of 2007 would see a major change at the football club, as the successful Southampton businessman Marcus Hackney took over as Chairman. Hackney was a close friend of Baird's, who had previously not taken too much interest in football:

"I had been involved with Havant & Waterlooville for a year or two before taking up the role as Chairman. I was going through a divorce and it was Bairdy who persuaded me to go to watch a game one Saturday afternoon, just to get me out of the house. It became a regular thing and, after getting to know the Directors and sponsoring the club, I was asked by Derek Pope if I was interested in replacing the outgoing Pete Demott and becoming the Chairman. It was a massive step, having only gone down there to relieve the boredom."

On the field, Baird had to rally the troops for the new season. The defeat in the play-offs had to be forgotten, as the players prepared for another nine months of long hard battle.

# 28

# Resignation, fall-out and rivalry

Havant suffered an indifferent start in the league, but the end of September brought a welcome respite in the form of the FA Cup. Having reached the first round proper in the previous season – where they were beaten 2-1 by Millwall in a game switched to Portsmouth's Fratton Park – the Hawks were looking to swell the coffers with another spirited cup run. Bognor Regis Town were the opposition, and a late Jamie Slabber header provided a passage into the third qualifying round.

With the FA Cup historically providing shocks year after year, Havant suffered a shock of a different nature on the morning after the Bognor game – when Baird informed Marcus Hackney that he was resigning as manager:

"Ian rang me on the Sunday morning to tell me that he was driving over to my house, as he needed to speak to me face to face. We sat in my living room, and he delivered the knockout blow that he was resigning to take up the role as manager of our arch-rivals Eastleigh.

"I was staggered; there was no changing his mind. Ian Baird was the man that had introduced me to the football club. I was more than happy with the job he was doing and the progress we were making. His knowledge of the game is second to none. His record at the club was pretty good and we were losing a fantastic manager. And I quickly realised that I faced a daunting task without my mate.

"We had got into a routine on a Saturday night. Bairdy, Adi Aymes and I would meet up in the local, discuss many topics and put the world to rights over a few pints. All that changed, and it was difficult to retain the friendship we had built. A lot of friction was generated. And looking back, I made a mistake and I should have left Havant & Waterlooville when Ian did."

In that part of the country, Havant & Waterlooville and Eastleigh are non-league football's equivalent of Portsmouth and Southampton, and Baird's decision to cross the divide to Eastleigh caused an incredible amount of bitterness and strife.

On the 1st of October 2007, Eastleigh Football Club issued a statement confirming that they had made an official approach to Havant & Waterlooville for permission to speak to Ian Baird, with a view to him becoming their first team manager.

With Ian being just two months into a three-year contract at Havant, the club had threatened to take out an injunction to block his move to Eastleigh. But following talks between Marcus Hackney, Derek Pope and the Eastleigh directors, the move was agreed. Eastleigh paid a £20,000 compensation fee for Baird's services, and he was appointed on the 3rd of October 2007.

Baird saw the move to Eastleigh as a natural progression in his development as a football manager:

"I was losing enthusiasm at Havant. The club had many problems off the field, the money was running out and I was fighting a losing battle. Eastleigh had been in contact with me and, after a thought process, I decided I wanted to go.

"The move caused uproar. I was referred to as 'Judas', but the truth is I didn't go for the money. In fact, I was on the same contract that I had been on at Havant. The move was purely down to footballing reasons.

"Upon leaving Havant, I felt let down by many people and friendships were affected. Some were even lost. Scandalous things were said about me, and I learnt a lot about people during that period."

Ian walked into his new club, and discovered a situation not too dissimilar to the one he had found at Havant. He felt some players were being massively overpaid, and not justifying their salaries with performances on the pitch.

Paul Doswell, who had been manager between 2002 and 2006, was a pivotal figure at the club – and from the start of the 2007-08 season he had been back in charge of first team affairs, along with David Hughes.

Baird felt that changes were needed, in the form of some new faces to ignite the club's season. In a bold move, he approached his former employers to sign players he knew he could put his faith in.

His daring raids did nothing but fuel the bitter fire that was burning between the fierce rivals. Goalkeeper Gareth Howells, midfielder Fitzroy Simpson, defender Tom Jordan and Matt Gray were all in Ian's sights. But Havant were making national headlines with an unbelievable cup run and Baird did not have things all his own way, especially in the pursuit of Tom Jordan:

"Ian had made me captain of Havant & Waterlooville at the start of his first full season. I was only 23 and that meant a lot to me. He had helped me develop as a player and I trusted his every word.

"When he arrived at Havant, we became a much more organised unit. We were stronger and fitter, and as a squad we pulled together and everybody worked for each other – which hadn't always been the case under the previous regime.

"Bairdy was generally a man of few words. He rarely showed any emotion and this kept us all on our toes. We would be trying to work out what he was thinking and how he felt about our performances.

"It was common knowledge in Hampshire that Ian wanted to take me to Eastleigh, but Havant were intent on keeping me. We had embarked on a fantastic run in the FA Cup, and had drawn 1-1 away at Swansea City in the third round proper.

"The draw had been made, and we knew that the winners of the replay would face a trip to Anfield to play Liverpool. I struck an agreement with the Chairman that if I helped the club beat Swansea, then I could join Eastleigh."

Tom Jordan was named as substitute on what turned out to be an incredible night for the non-league outfit. Havant raced into a 3-0 lead but goals either side of half-time brought Swansea back into the game – before the in-demand central defender entered the fray, and his goal sealed a brilliant 4-2 victory and a dream trip to Merseyside:

"Unfortunately, Havant didn't stick to their word. And I remained at the club until the end of the season, before finally signing for Bairdy and Eastleigh in the summer for a fee of £10,000."

On the day that Havant & Waterlooville travelled to Anfield, Ian Baird was stood on the touchline at Bognor Regis Town, in his capacity of Eastleigh manager. Ironically the same venue where the Hawks' cup run had started:

"We beat Bognor 3-0. But during the first half, news filtered through that Havant had taken the lead at Anfield. I have to admit to being a bit envious. There was I thinking I had fucked up again and that the grass wasn't always greener."

The grass certainly wasn't greener on the 22nd of December, when Ian returned to Havant to see his Eastleigh side lose 1-0 to an 87th minute header from substitute Chamal Fenelon.

Ian admits that life at Eastleigh was tough. He had been under the impression that Paul Doswell had stepped aside but that wasn't the case:

"Doswell had put so much time, effort and money into the club and all wasn't what it had seemed. At Havant I had been the manager, and there were no interferences from anybody when it came down to football matters. At Eastleigh, I found it difficult to work with Doswell. But saying that, he was very supportive when it came to the club providing the funds to try and get us into the play-offs.

"I brought Fitzroy Simpson and Gareth Howells into the club, along with left back, Adam Everitt. Goalkeeper David Wilkinson came in on loan from Crystal Palace, and Mark Marshall signed a permanent deal following his loan spell from Grays Athletic."

Other players were brought in as Baird looked to achieve the objective of getting his new side into the play-offs.

Eastleigh's quest was hampered by a bad run towards the end of the season, when they picked up just three points from four games. One of those points came courtesy of a late Paul Sales goal in a home draw with Havant, on the occasion of Baird's 44th birthday.

Despite a 3-2 defeat at lowly St Albans, the Spitfires knew that a victory at Thurrock on the final day would guarantee a place in the play-offs. But the day didn't go to plan:

"I had a feeling that if we failed to win then, there would be a real knock-on effect. It was a tough time for the economy, and on the morning of the game a major sponsor had informed us that they were pulling out.

"Thurrock were mid-table with nothing to play for but, like any side in that league, they could turn it on when they wanted to. I made a mistake of playing Fitzroy Simpson who wasn't 100% fit, when I should have played David Hughes. Anthony Riviere was sent off for handball and, although our goalkeeper Jason Matthews saved the penalty, we were beaten 4-1."

Having occupied a play-off place for 10 weeks, Eastleigh had missed out on the final day and faced another season in the Blue Square South league:

"It was one of those bitterly disappointing days that football throws up. In the car on the way back to Hampshire, I thought Doswell was going to drive off the bridge going over the Dartford crossing. I could see how disappointed he was. He had put his heart and soul into the club and his contribution had been immense."

Just four days after the defeat at Thurrock, Paul Doswell announced in a shock move that he was quitting Eastleigh Football Club. He would leave his role as co-assistant manager to Ian Baird, and also his position on the Board as an equity director:

"Without Paul Doswell and his money, if it hadn't been for Paul Murray and Dave Malone, the football club would have folded. The budget for the following season was cut in half. But personally it was good for me that Doswell had gone, for reasons I have already mentioned."

Despite the financial cut-backs, Baird managed to sign Matt Groves, Tom Jordan, Trevor Challis, James Baker and Tony Taggart, with many players leaving the club to balance the books.

"We had a good pre-season – which included a 3-3 draw against a young Southampton side before we won the Errea Cup, a tournament held in Devon in which we beat Torquay United on penalties in the final."

The new season got underway on the 9th of August. A Luke Byles header sealed an opening-day win at Thurrock, the scene of so much despair just a few months earlier. To highlight the amount of changes over the summer, only five players started both of those games in an Eastleigh shirt.

Despite a steady start to the season, the club was still looking to reduce its running costs. In October David Hughes left by mutual consent, and further cost-cutting measures were to follow:

"Our budget was dependant on success in the Cups, the FA Cup and the FA Trophy – and unfortunately we were eliminated from both competitions early on. This affected the playing staff, and Dave Malone conducted a presentation to the players which detailed why they would all have to take a 20% pay cut. It was serious stuff but the mood was lifted when Jamie Brown, looking rather concerned, asked if the 20% included VAT.

"We had a great run at the end of the season. The place was galvanised and, due to the problems that Southampton were experiencing, our attendances were on the up. The football club was a great place to be. Everybody pulled together and there were a lot of good people around, including Denis Bundy in the Commercial Department, Steve Brookwell, Phil Pairpoint and Pat Mallon who sold the lottery tickets."

Phil Pairpoint, a mate of Matt Gray's, was brought in by Matt to help out with the training sessions, the pre-match warm-ups and the post-match warm-downs. Phil recalled the day he was introduced to the squad by Baird:

"Ian told the players, 'Today is bring-a-friend day. Matt Gray has brought in his mate Pairsy who will be helping us out'. The players absolutely hammered me to start with, but it worked out well. I loved being involved, and it didn't take long for me to realise how intense and passionate Bairdy was."

On the 26th of March Ian signed a contract extension until 2011, which highlighted how well he had done in his first full season. It brought a new-found stability to the club:

"We were flying – and of the final nine games of the season, we won seven and drew one. Wimbledon were the biggest draw in the league that season and, at the end of March, a crowd of 2,283 packed into the Silverlake Stadium to see us beat them 2-1. Tom Jordan scored the first with his hand, and the only two people in the ground that failed to spot it were the referee and his assistant."

Many predicted Eastleigh would go on and win the title, but that wasn't to be. They finished in third place, five points behind Wimbledon who were promoted as Champions. A two-legged play-off against Hayes & Yeading would follow. In the other play-off semi-final, Hampton & Richmond faced Chelmsford City.

The Spitfires travelled to West London for the first leg to face Hayes & Yeading, who themselves had been on a tremendous run.

"Our performance that night, for the first 70 minutes, was the best I got out of a side during my management career. We were absolutely superb."

Tony Taggart put Baird's charges 1-0 up after just five minutes, and 60 seconds later they were awarded a penalty from which Taggart was denied. Brett Williams made it 2-0 after 26 minutes and right on half-time, Anthony Riviere made it 3-0. Another goal followed just six minutes after the restart, when Williams grabbed his second and Eastleigh's fourth.

Eastleigh were in dreamland. A blistering display had seen them take full control of the tie. But a penalty and a last-minute header saw the home side reduce the arrears:

"Everybody was talking about the final. Hampton & Richmond had won 3-1 at Chelmsford. And should they complete the job, the final was scheduled to be at their ground – courtesy of them finishing the highest in the league out of the four teams involved.

"The match day programme for our second-leg tie gave the directions to Hampton & Richmond's ground. As soon as I saw it, I knew the omens were not good. And sure enough, the dreaded 'Ian Baird bad luck' struck again."

After 12 minutes Riviere saw a volley come back off the post, before he went off injured nine minutes later. Eastleigh suffered another blow when the influential Brett Williams went off injured at half-time. Due to the budget cuts, Baird had limited options sitting on the bench.

Hayes & Yeading took the lead on the stroke of half-time, and forced extra-time courtesy of a hotly disputed penalty with nine minutes of normal time remaining.

Two further goals followed for the visitors – who recorded a remarkable 6-4 aggregate win, after being 4-0 down at one stage. To rub salt into the wounds, Tony Taggart missed another penalty. But in reality the tie was already over as a contest:

"I remember the first goal. They had a succession of corners and my goalkeeper Jason Matthews, who had been brilliant for me, misjudged the flight of the ball which ended up in the back of the net.

"The players came in at half-time and I knew they had gone. I could see it in their eyes. The dressing room was like a morgue.

"At full-time, I was deflated. I felt sick and struggled to come to terms with it all. I knew we had missed a golden opportunity and the players knew it too. Some of them were in tears. I went away on holiday during the summer but couldn't get it out of my system, and I was dreading going back to the club for pre-season training."

# 29

# A brief comeback then goodbye

An agreement had been in place from earlier in the season that if the club qualified for the play-offs, they would be rewarded with a four-day break to Spain. The club was true to their word and a great time was had by all. Gareth Howells, the club's goalkeeper, remembers the trip well:

"One morning, Bairdy was up and about at ten o'clock. Despite the fact that we had been out the previous day and had plenty of drink, he was raring to go again.

"We consumed an early lunch and were soon back on the beer. I remember Bairdy sticking a toothpick in Matt Gray's head, before two of us had to carry him out of the toilets in Linekers Bar."

Another incident involving Baird was recalled by Jamie Brown:

"We were sat drinking at a beach bar – there was Bairdy, Andy Harris, Matt Gray, Phil Pairpoint and I. The banter was in full swing and all of a sudden Bairdy asked me to punch him the stomach. He tensed up and I hit him, he took the punch well and asked me to hit him again. So I gave him my best, and he took that.

"When Bairdy asked me to punch him for a third time, Pairsy stepped in and stopped it, knowing it was a bad idea. In hindsight it was a good job that Pairsy intervened as, a few days later, Bairdy started pissing blood."

The 2009-10 season proved to be a disappointing one for all concerned with Eastleigh. After an inconsistent campaign, the club finished in 11th place and like all managers, Baird had his ups and downs:

"I brought in Michael Gosney on loan from AFC Totton. The deal was for an initial one-month period, and Gosney made his debut as a substitute away at Thurrock but then was never seen again.

"The lad failed to turn up for training – and despite Matt Gray, Dave Malone and myself trying to contact him; he never answered any of our calls.

"Malone then received a text message from Gosney, explaining he had work commitments. But I made the decision that he wouldn't be involved with us again. He seemed a decent lad and he had ability, but I wasn't going to pick a player who failed to turn up for training without a prior agreement."

It was a mixed start to the season for the club. Following a 5-1 defeat at Newport County, Baird told his players that their heads and his own head were on the block:

"I was a manager who was loyal to his players, and providing they did the business for me I would defend them and do my best for them. But after that defeat at Newport, it was impossible to defend them. The money was no longer available to go out and buy new players, I had to work with what I had and it was proving increasingly difficult."

On the 6th of October 2009, Eastleigh travelled to Christchurch for a Hampshire Senior Cup tie. With several players unavailable, it was an unfamiliar side which took to the field.

Andy Cook, the physiotherapist and ex-professional player, made a cameo appearance – and wearing the number nine shirt, at the age of 45 years old, was Ian Baird. Eastleigh lost the game 2-1 after extra-time. But Ian admits he quite enjoyed the experience, despite the result:

"It was nice to get the boots on again and, although you never lose your footballing brain or your ability, it is your legs that go. It took me a few days to get over it, and I could have done with spraying a can of WD40 on my legs to get them going again."

Baird always kept himself in good shape, and was keen to take part in games played during training sessions. These games would be refereed by his assistant manager Matt Gray:

"Bairdy was comical. He knew his legs had gone, but he would drift over to the left-hand side despite being all right-footed. When he received the ball he would cut inside, and if he got the slightest touch he would go to ground claiming a free kick but I would always wave play on.

"If the side that Bairdy was on won the game, he was unbearable. He would hang around and take the piss out of the lads on the opposition, and he'd score himself a steady 7 out of 10 for his performance.

"However, when he was on the losing side he would storm back to the changing room and not speak to anybody. When the rest of us got back in, Bairdy would be showered and changed. He'd always blame me for being a useless referee, he would brand me a disgrace. He hated losing."

October 2009 brought a welcome break from the pressures of management, as the club sanctioned Ian, Matt Gray, Phil Pairpoint and Andy Cook to go back to Spain for four days on a staff teambuilding exercise. Matt Gray will always remember a couple of incidents:

"We stayed in Bairdy's apartment, which is situated at the top of a steep hill. At the bottom of this hill you will find an Irish bar, and one day we had spent a considerable amount of time in there.

"Several beers and been downed and we had eaten quite a large amount of food. We were chatting away and exchanging banter, when all of a sudden Bairdy started a debate with me on who had been the most successful England manager – Bobby Robson or Terry Venables.

"I knew Bairdy would plump for Bobby so I said Venables. It sparked a 20-minute row, and Bairdy was getting angry. He jumped up, smashed his glass, stormed outside, got in his car and drove back to his apartment.

"In all honesty, I knew he wasn't too concerned about the England managers. It was his way of getting out of paying towards the huge bar tab we had run up. Cooky, Pairsy and I were left to settle the bill, but what pissed the three of us off the most was the fact that we had to walk back up the hill.

"Another sizeable bar tab was racked up following a round of golf at the Los Arqueros Golf and Country Club. The course was designed by Severiano Ballesteros and is set among the mountains.

"Having driven there in a four-seater van, we teed off at lunchtime. And by darkness, we had drank about 10 pints each and between us polished off a couple of bottles of wine in the club house. We were in a fair old state, especially Pairsy who had lost the ability to speak.

"Bairdy came out of the toilets and suggested to me, as I had the 'whip', that we did a runner without settling the bar tab. In a bid to get to the van, he and

Cooky ran up the stairs and through the actual bar – when all they had to do was walk round the corner and the van was there.

"In his drunken state, and due to the fact it was pitch black, Bairdy ran straight past the van as about eight waiters – who probably had an idea of what was happening – came walking around the corner.

"Eventually we all piled into the van. And in a frantic attempt to get away, rather than find reverse, Bairdy put the vehicle into first gear and drove straight through a hedge. In the end, I was steering and Bairdy was controlling the pedals. In the back seats sat Cooky, who was egging Ian on to go harder on the accelerator, and poor old Pairsy who sat there licking the windows.

"We endured a 15-minute nightmare journey through the windy mountain roads and that experience soon sobered me up."

With the club being knocked out of the Hampshire Senior Cup, it was in the FA Cup that Eastleigh would excel. After wins over Witney United, Basingstoke Town and Dover Athletic, the club reached the first round proper for the first time in its history. They faced Barrow, a division above the Spitfires in the non-league pyramid. But despite dominating the game they were beaten 2-1, with the winning goal coming deep into time added on. It was more heartache for Baird,

"We totally dominated the game, and I really felt for the players at the end. Every single player put in a great performance and the very least we deserved was a draw. Once again, we had to bounce back from a cruel defeat."

Eastleigh were left with a fixture pile-up, as a result of the original schedule falling foul to the winter weather. But it was a very heated afternoon at the end of January when Baird renewed rivalries with his former club Havant:

"I made the headlines that day for refusing to shake hands with the opposing manager Shaun Gale, who had been my assistant during my tenure as manager of Havant. When questioned by the local media, I replied that Shaun wasn't my cup of tea and I refrained from saying anymore.

"In fairness, it was all done in the heat of the moment. There was an intense rivalry between the clubs and, in hindsight, I regret that particular incident."

With the games coming thick and fast, Eastleigh found themselves in 11$^{th}$ place towards the end of February after an 8-2 home defeat by Thurrock. Questions were asked of Baird and he knew the pressure was on:

"I still couldn't get the play-off defeat out of my system, and I began to lose some of my enthusiasm for the job. I felt that the pressure was beginning to mount and I was far from enjoying it."

Director of Football Dave Malone defended Baird, and his faith was repaid with three consecutive away wins that took the club into the play-off places. But with home wins hard to come by and two defeats over Easter, the play-off dream vanished and Eastleigh finished the season 11th in the league table.

Baird set about making the necessary changes to improve the squad. Brett Williams, who had been sold during the previous season, returned to the club (he would be sold on again to Championship side Reading). He was followed by Will Hendry, who had played a pivotal role in Hayes & Yeading's remarkable play-off victory over Eastleigh at the end of the 2008-09 season.

Hendry originally signed on a non-contract basis. But after playing a handful of games, the deal was made permanent. But it was a move that didn't work out, and Hendry was soon released after a breach of club discipline:

"There was no doubting his ability, but I felt he wasn't a team player and advised him to take up golf or tennis. He was substitute for a game against Dartford and I sent him on with just a few minutes remaining.

"It was customary for the subs to go back onto the pitch with Matt Gray to do some exercise in a bid to keep their fitness levels up. But he refused, telling Matt that he hadn't joined the club to sit on the bench and not play. That was the end of his time at Eastleigh. I had no room in my squad for players with that sort of attitude.

"Besides that, it was a difficult period. As a manager, it's not just about the training and the games; you have to deal with all the other shit that comes with the job. All sorts of people within the club have their own ideas on how things should be done, and it invents pressure.

"However, at that level of football you are relying on the generosity of the directors – and when they are pumping their own money in, they want their opinions to be heard. It's a case of having to bite your tongue and get on with it, because 99 times out of a 100 you don't agree with their opinions and what they have to say.

"I had been dealing mainly with Dave Malone, and we had a decent relationship. The best way to describe Malone is that he is a 'likeable prick'.

"He would help me out and fight my corner. But we had our bust ups, and I should have been sacked after one time when we had a standing argument over the signing of a player and I threatened to fill him in.

"Our relationship began to break down when I discovered that Eastleigh had spoken to ex-Southampton player Tommy Widdrington about my job. I went absolutely ballistic and it was another chance they had to sack me, because in the heat of the moment I said some unforgiveable things. But I knew that I held the cards, as I was under contract and the team were on a half decent run and playing well."

Progress was made in the FA Cup, but unfortunately the Spitfires fell at the final hurdle. They were denied entry into the first round proper following an unfortunate defeat at Woking where, despite goals from Richard Gillespie and Jamie Slabber, Baird's men bowed out with a 3-2 defeat:

"After losing at Woking we went on a great run, and were beaten just once in 14 games in all competitions. But we suffered a huge blow in the FA Trophy when Chasetown, who were a league below us, beat us 2-1 at the Silverlake Stadium."

With the falling-out put to bed, Baird – who had offered to resign on three occasions – signed a new two-year contract. Dave Malone admitted the club wanted stability, and they felt that progress was being made under Ian's management:

"We were 8th in the league and just four points of the play-offs, with games in hand. Having looked at all our options, we agreed that Ian Baird was the man to take us forward and build for the future."

Despite being in a great position, Eastleigh endured a bad run towards the end of the season and finished the campaign in 8th place with 72 points. But there was real cause for optimism when the club announced it was going full-time and plans were in place to build a young squad in a fresh approach to achieve the long-term aim of promotion:

"We planned on recruiting young players who had been released by Football League clubs. Each year there are loads of young players, who all have preconceived ideas about their futures. They have agents promising that they can do this and that, but in reality they are struggling to come to terms with being thrown onto the scrap heap.

"It takes them time to recover and decide on their futures, so we knew we had to be patient."

Following the failure to get into the play-offs, Eastleigh released 9 members of the squad. In addition Luke Byles was due to return to Australia, Chris Holland had rejected a new deal and Tony Taggart had been offered a deal at Sutton United.

Baird's new look side started the season in the worst possible fashion with three defeats on the bounce, before earning an impressive point against title favourites Woking.

Despite the club going full-time, money remained hard to come by. Then in November, the club recommended that its shareholders should accept an offer from Oxford-based Bridle Insurance Limited for the purchase of a majority shareholding.

Just before Christmas, 2011 Eastleigh announced that the deal was complete, subject to the necessary paperwork. Stewart Donald and Neil Fox had been elected as Directors of the football club, and Paul Murray would remain as Non-Executive Chairman:

"Glenn Hoddle's football academy had been using Eastleigh Football Club as a vehicle for its young talent. A few players had come in and hardly set the place alight, and overall the academy was failing. Hoddle looked to Stewart Donald and Bridle Insurance for investment, but somehow Dave Malone managed to intervene and he swerved them towards Eastleigh in what was a real masterstroke."

Bridle Insurance did not hesitate in providing transfer funds – and a deal was agreed to sign the highly-rated Bognor Regis striker Jason Prior, who had plundered 92 goals in 120 games. Prior, whose progress was being monitored by several Football League clubs, would become Eastleigh's record signing in a £12,000 swoop.

The deal fell through in a cruel twist however, as Prior had been invited to train with Premier League side Newcastle United with a view to a possible transfer. After Eastleigh had announced the deal was all but done, some backtracking was required. It left a few people disappointed that their record deal was off, but not the manager:

"In honesty, although Malone was keen, I didn't want to sign the lad. I was wary of the whole situation and I knew that if I splashed out that amount of money and things went pear-shaped, everyone would point the finger at me."

On the field, Baird's side were progressing in the Hampshire Senior Cup. Victory over Romsey Town saw them take their place in the semi-final against Winchester City.

In a game littered with bookings, a late Jamie Slabber penalty saw Eastleigh book their place in the final, where they would face AFC Totton. It was a remarkable turnaround:

"In the earlier rounds, we had been drawn away at Aldershot and lost 4-1. The Shots went on to play Farnborough who they beat 2-1. It transpired that Aldershot had fielded an ineligible player in both ties, against Farnborough and Eastleigh. They were charged with the offence and removed from the competition.

"The drama didn't end there. Farnborough also admitted to playing with ineligible players in their second-round tie against Fleet Town, and they too were kicked out of the competition. Fleet, along with ourselves, were reinstated and played each other in round three."

The cup run proved a welcome break from the league campaign, in which by mid-March play-off hopes were fading fast. By the end of the month, those hopes were over after a humiliating 6-1 defeat at Boreham Wood.

Fans on the internet message boards were calling for Baird to be sacked. Despite being told by the new owners that he would be judged the following season, Baird had his concerns:

"I was embarrassed by that defeat, and I told the media that I thought the players had thrown the towel in due to what was going on at the club.

"Stewart Donald wanted to bring in his mate Richard Hill as my assistant but, following a meeting with Richard, we both knew that it wasn't feasible. However, I knew that Richard Hill would become the new manager once Donald and the Board were presented with the first opportunity to sack me, and it was a very unsettling time."

Eastleigh finished the season in 12th place. But they had the consolation of lifting the Hampshire Senior Cup after a 2-0 win over AFC Totton at Southampton's St Mary's Stadium, with goals from Chris Flood and Mitchell Nelson. Tom Jordan lifted the trophy but Baird was absent:

"After the defeat to Aldershot earlier in the tournament, I committed to going to the Hong Kong International Soccer Sevens. I was sorry to miss the final but I left the situation in Shaun Wilkinson's capable hands."

After a hectic pre-season on the transfer front, Baird saw his side made promotion favourites by the bookmakers. He warned that Rome wasn't built in a day, and there was some real hard work ahead for everybody connected with the club.

Unfortunately, the club didn't get off to the best of starts and on the 11th of September 2012, Eastleigh relieved Ian Baird from his position as first team manager following a 4-0 defeat at Billericay. Not surprisingly, he was replaced by Richard Hill – whose appointment was confirmed within 24 hours of Ian leaving the club,

"Like I said, I knew I was on a sticky wicket and I had been for sometime. But I fully believe that the reason I got the sack was predominantly because of Richard Hill and his friendship with Stewart Donald.

"Saying that, I don't hold any grudges against the two of them because these things happen in football. I had been given a fantastic budget and we'd had a good pre-season, but after a disappointing start I was gone. My ambition had been to take Eastleigh higher but I never managed to do that.

"In addition, I was extremely disappointed for the club and the supporters at the end of the 2012-13 season when they failed to get promotion, having lost in the play-offs."

# 30

## Never say never

Off the field, Ian has always tried to enjoy himself and live life to the full. Ever since his childhood he has spent a lot of time over in Spain – and jaunts with his mates during his early days at Southampton were always typically eventful young lads' holidays, providing great memories for Ian and the pals that accompanied him.

Ian is the father of two children, Amy and Liam, who were born during his first marriage to Lesley Lowman.

Before conceiving with Amy, Lesley had fallen pregnant but the couple were devastated when she lost the baby, only eight weeks before she was due to give birth:

"It was a real nightmare. I received a phone call at Elland Road whilst I was training, and I was informed that Lesley was bleeding. I rushed straight back to be with her, but unfortunately she lost the baby. Thankfully, at the time we had her parents staying with us who were very supportive.

"The baby had been planned, we had everything ready and it was a truly shattering time for us."

Soon after the heartbreak, Ian was on the move to Portsmouth. The couple sold up to return to Hampshire.

It was during Ian's ill-fated spell at Portsmouth that their first child Amy was born – on the 27th of October 1987, just three days after Ian had scored his only goal for the south-coast club:

"Amy being born was amazing for us, especially after the miscarriage. I have always been a squeamish person and I could never imagine watching a baby coming out of a woman. So I decided to stay in the hospital waiting room, watching *Neighbours* on the television whilst Lesley gave birth.

"You hear of players missing games to be at the birth of their children, but that wasn't for me. As much I love my children, I couldn't have watched it all unfold.

"The first time I saw Alan Ball after the birth, he expressed how delighted he was for Lesley and I. He welcomed me into a 'man's world', now that I had become a father."

The family would soon be back on the move, when Billy Bremner rescued the burly striker from his nightmare spell on the south coast. The family were ecstatic, and Lesley admits that the best times of Ian's career were whilst he was playing for Leeds United.

On the 19th of May 1990, Ian's son Liam was born, and the couple could have not have been happier:

"All was well at home and Liam came along in May, just after we had escaped relegation at Middlesbrough with that fantastic win over Newcastle United. But again, I didn't want to witness the birth – and as Liam was being delivered, I was asleep in the waiting room at Sheffield Hospital."

Liam is a Leeds United fan but as a commercial diver, often working across Europe, his occupational demands prevent him from getting to Elland Road as often as he would like. It is a job that Liam modestly describes as being 'an underwater labourer'. He enjoys football and, when his dad was manager at Havant & Waterlooville, Liam would take part in the training sessions and help out with general duties around the club.

Following his divorce from Lesley, Ian met Christina Bogatto on a blind date arranged by one of Christina's friends. The pair married in August 2002.

For Ian's 40th birthday in 2004, Christina took him for a surprise one-week stay in Las Vegas. But another holiday to Dubai caused her both concern and amusement:

"We were sat round the pool on the last day of the holiday, and for the evening I had planned a romantic meal with cocktails.

"I went up to the room to pack the bags for the following day's journey home, leaving Ian at the poolside. He was speaking to a bloke we had met, who he had nicknamed 'Azerbaijan Tony'. Tony had ordered a bottle of champagne, and by 7pm I was waiting for Ian to return to the room.

"I was still waiting an hour later, all ready to go for the meal. I looked out onto the beach and could see a lone figure staggering across the sand, falling over deckchairs. I soon realised it was Ian who then, in his drunken state, wandered into the sea and had to be rescued by the lifeguards."

Christina's daughter Jessica is the mother of two children, Neo and Dexter, who Ian spends a lot of time with. Neo is a budding young footballer, who receives plenty of encouragement from Ian.

At the tender age of 45, Ian – who has always kept himself in good shape – decided to enter the ring for a charity white-collar fight on an evening of pugilism.

The ring announcer was Denis Bundy, the compère and comedian. Denis also worked as the Marketing Manager for Eastleigh Football Club, and he is a man who Ian looks on as a father figure.

Though Denis admits that Ian can be a nightmare at times, they go back a long way. And he is always willing to offer his advice on any issues that may be bothering Ian:

"It was a fantastic occasion when Bairdy stepped into the ring. He took the whole thing very seriously, and he wanted to win. He trained hard, worked the pads and went on to show that he was a pretty strong boxer.

"His opponent was in his late 20s. He knew of Bairdy's stature as an ex-professional footballer, and he wanted to hurt him. It would have been a nice scalp for the lad. Bairdy, who suffered a couple of cuts, gave as good as he got. The pair put on a good show for a packed audience, and the end result was a creditable draw – although it's fair to say that after the three two-minute rounds, he was knackered."

It wasn't the first time that a Baird had entered a boxing ring. Ian's son Liam was a promising amateur boxer, who won two of his three fights:

"When Dad was training for his white-collar fight, we would train together down the gym. During one session, on a wintery day, we were going through the routine on the pads and doing some skipping.

"I accused Dad of not training hard enough and, in hindsight, it wasn't a wise move. He went ballistic and after the workout, he drove home on his own, leaving me to run the 10 miles in the snow wearing just a tee-shirt and tracksuit bottoms."

It wasn't the first time that Liam had fallen foul of his Dad's competitive nature: "At the age of 14, whilst away in Spain, Dad and I decided to play a round of golf every day for five days and see who won at the end of it. Dad would try and put me off every shot and give me a bit of stick, and at times I struggled to handle the banter. However, after four days we had both won two games.

"On the deciding day, we were on the 18th and Dad needed to putt to win. He missed and I burst out laughing, he chased me around the green waving the putter about and made me walk back to the villa."

Although Liam played football on a Sunday morning, he had no ambition to follow in his father's footsteps. Ian would go and watch Liam play, but during one game he witnessed his son overstep the mark:

"I was on the touchline, Liam was getting upset with the referee, and he was giving him plenty of backchat. I then heard him swear at the ref – so I walked onto the pitch, took Liam by the scruff of the neck and made him sit in the car, hoping it would teach him a valuable lesson."

Cricket is another sport in which Ian takes a watching interest. When living in Yorkshire, annual trips to Headingly for an England test match were very much on the agenda.

Nick Buxton, a friend of Ian's, remembers one particular trip to the home of Yorkshire cricket:

"On a regular basis we would take in the test match. There would be a few of us – including Bairdy, Mouthy Mick Inman, the Big Bird (John Pearson), my father (Richard Buxton), John Spiers, Big Duncan Haigue, Del Boy (Deryck Crossland) and Giuseppe (Paul Trainer). Armed with carrier bags full of alcohol, we would travel by train from Chapeltown, north Sheffield, into Leeds knowing we were in for a great day.

"On one occasion the morning session was cancelled due to the weather. So we all decided to take cover in the nearest beer tent, and the day was mapped out from there.

"Bairdy fancied his chances drinking with Big Del Boy, a former professional cricketer who stood 6 foot 8 and weighed around 18 stones. He was a regular 15 pint per session man, but Bairdy was up for the challenge.

"By half past two it was carnage, and a few of us were starting to see things before us that were not there. We had a few more pints in the ground, and all staggered to a nearby pub for more beer.

"We boarded the six o'clock train and all got a seat, Bairdy was sat across from me and my dad, and we were accompanied by Paul Trainer. After a session on the beer, Trainer would always fall asleep, and again he did so. He was sporting a brand new pair of shoes which Bairdy removed from his feet and threw them out of the moving train's window. The whole carriage was laughing, and it wasn't until Trainer woke up at the end of the journey that he realised he had no shoes on.

"In the end, we all decided on another drink at *Scandals* in Chapeltown, Bairdy got us all in free, but Trainer had no shoes so they refused him entrance. As we were drinking in the pub, he sat outside for over an hour waiting for us. It was typical Bairdy."

Matt Gray, Ian's former assistant at Eastleigh, recalls a time when he was on the receiving end of Bairdy's wicked sense of humour:

"I had agreed to go on a date with a friend of Christina's, and naively gave the thumbs up for Ian and Christina to join us. As I already stated, I do not eat hot spicy food and Bairdy knew this fact.

"Unbelievably, I let him choose where we would go and eat and he booked a table at a Thai restaurant. I knew he was trying to stitch me up, he was succeeding and things got worse.

"When the waiter came over to take our order, Bairdy and the two ladies agreed, against my wishes, that we should obtain several different dishes and between us we could sample a bit of each.

"Bairdy did me up good and proper. He ordered a mountain of hot spicy Thai food, and was encouraging me to try it. With the pressure mounting, I tasted some of the curry and immediately I starting burning up. The sweat was running from my bald head, and Bairdy was pissing himself laughing across the table. He even called the waiter over to ask him if there was a leak coming from the ceiling, due to the fact that my head was soaking wet."

Ian is a big fan of international football, and has followed England to several major international tournaments. His business partner Russell

Vaughan, along with Hayden and Leroy Whale, accompanied Ian on a trip to Portugal for the 2004 European Championship finals:

"We were in a bar and Bairdy was having a debate with the businessman Adam Pearson, who was the chairman of Hull City. The debate centred on the Hull manager Peter Taylor, who in Bairdy's view was overrated.

"As Pearson left the bar, he forgot to pick up his mobile phone which he had left on the table. Bairdy picked it up, and soon enough, Pearson – realising his mistake – was trying to call the phone from another one he owned.

"Bairdy answered it, speaking in an Eastern European accent, demanding €300 for the return of the phone. Pearson was panicking – he had no idea it was Bairdy and he was even replying to his demands in broken English, trying to get his point across.

"Two years later, a trip was arranged to go to Germany during the World Cup. England were playing Trinidad & Tobago at the Frankenstadion in Nuremberg, and we hired a four-seater plane to make the journey. The pilot couldn't land in the main airport as the flight path was hectic, but he managed to obtain permission to land at a small private airfield.

"The flight was horrendous, and we were on edge for the whole journey. It didn't help matters when the pilot asked Bairdy, mid-flight, to make sure the door was closed."

Ian's football career has been a long history of ups and downs, highs and lows. He has encountered his fair share of bad luck; he's also had his fair share of run-ins with the governing bodies, due to his disciplinary problems. However, he has always given his all and he demanded the same effort from those around him.

After being dismissed from his duties as Eastleigh manager, Ian managed to keep himself busy. Visits to the gym became more regular and, although he initially turned down offers of corporate tickets to football matches, he was soon back into the swing of things.

He found employment working as a player's agent for Midas Sports. But, although he enjoyed the work and got on well with the owner Steve Wood, he has recently left the position:

"Steve is a top guy, but let's just say that he is the boss and he likes things to be done his way. I am pretty headstrong and I have my own way of doing things, and I don't always like being told what to do. I felt it was best that we parted company and went our separate ways."

Each year, Ian takes a team of veterans over to Hong Kong, where they participate in the Hong Kong International Soccer Sevens tournament. It is an event he always looks forward to and recently he has turned out for the Southampton ex-players association although he admits that it took him a few days to get over the experience due to his knee and ankle problems .

When asked the question as to whether he will ever make a return to football management, Ian replied, "Never say never".

Most of the people within the game that have contributed to Ian's story have declared that football needs Ian Baird – with the knowledge, ability, experience, passion and enthusiasm that he brings to the table. Some people may not agree, but ask any Leeds United supporter who witnessed the 1980s and they certainly will.

Thanks for the memories Bairdy and good luck for the future

# The fans' view

When Ian agreed to my suggestion of putting together his life story, I offered the supporters of all the clubs that he had played for the chance to have their recollections of Ian included in the book.

Ian himself asked for this chapter of the book to be dedicated to the supporters of all the clubs he played for and managed who are no longer with us:

Special mentions for Christopher Loftus, Kevin Speight, Brendan O'Connor and Ian Hambridge.

Also, Kevin Jinks who, through former Leeds player Dylan Kerr, became a good friend of Ian's. Kevin was a huge help providing me with his own memories of Ian.

Tragically, Kevin passed away just weeks before I sent the first draft of this book to the publisher.

Thank you to everybody who took the time to contact me. Here are the anecdotes I chose.

### Kevin Jinks R.I.P, Leeds United fan

"I was lucky enough to see Ian make his home debut against Barnsley in 1985. I was 16 years old and stood on the Kop with my Uncle, who turned to me and told me that this is the type of player we had been missing.

"I was devastated when he left for Portsmouth but I witnessed his return to Leeds and the debut goal against Plymouth Argyle.

"After watching Leeds draw 0-0 in a dreadful game at Port Vale in 1989, I raced back to meet Dylan Kerr as we were having a few beers in Sheffield. That is the night I met Bairdy; he was a great character and rather than play up to the fact he was a professional footballer, he acted just like one of the lads. I wasn't kept at arm's length or treated like a star-struck fan, we became good friends and he nicknamed me 'luvly jubbly' due to my cockney ways.

"Ian is a true gentleman and I know for a fact that he is still held in great esteem by Leeds United supporters. I am lucky enough to be able to say that Ian is my mate and for that, I will always be grateful."

**Richard Hargrave, Leeds United fan**
"Ian Baird was, for me as a teenager in the mid 1980's, right up there with those players who have legendary status at Elland Road. During those dark days, I used to love watching him give everything for the cause."

**Michael Durkin, Leeds United fan**
"Queens Park Rangers from the First Division against a side that had spent 5 years in the doldrums (though improving under Billy) – we had no chance.

"I was a teenager at the time, so I would say that Baird's goal that day was one of those goals that gave me the bug to continue and for all bar two seasons, I have been a Kop season ticket holder ever since.

"I remember Bairdy scoring to put us 1-0 up and then the noise. It is one of those goals that always stick in the memory forever. It proves to be a defining moment from which you dedicate yourself to a football club. Yeboah v Liverpool, Sheridan v Charlton (despite the result), Sheffield United's own goal in 1992, Beckford at Old Trafford and Bairdy v Queens Park Rangers – Never to be forgotten."

**Martin Gale, Southampton fan**
"In 1996 I joined a Sunday league team who played in the Southampton pub league under the name of Willy's Bar Nomads. Willy's Bar was a wine bar on The Avenue in Southampton, owned by Ian Baird and Ian Leigh.

"The two Ians were involved with the team, Baird was playing for Brighton at the time and he was manager, whilst Leigh, an ex professional goalkeeper with Bournemouth, played in midfield.

"As a Southampton fan, I knew of Ian Baird and it was quite surreal him being manager of the team I played for.

"It was a professional-like set up, you were fined if you were late on match-day. Alan Murray, an ex Southampton coach used to help out and we won the league quite easily. Darren Baird played, Ian's brother, he was a fantastic player at that level. I was goalkeeper and by far the youngest member of the side. I didn't have the best of starts, in terms of performances but despite this, Bairdy never gave me a hard time, he was always encouraging me and at the end of the season, I won the award for most improved player. Bairdy had arranged for Saints players, Robbie Slater and Claus Lundekvam to come along and present the trophies, it was a great night.

"After every game, we would all pile into cars and head back to the bar, the first pint was always on the house and it was the little things like that which made you want to do well for the team.

"I remember one journey back to the bar, one of the players driving the car in front of mine, started swerving across the road; it was like he was losing control. Bairdy, travelling in my car, was pissing himself laughing. He'd put a very strong liniment in the lad's boxer shorts!"

### Matt Thompson, Leeds United fan
"As a youngster, me and a couple of pals used to go watch Leeds train on Fullerton Park hoping to get a few autographs. One day the three of us ventured onto the area next to where the players were training and after a while (waiting to see if we'd get moved on or not) started a game of headers and volleys in a real 'jumpers for goalposts' style with a miniature ball. A couple of passes from Leeds players strayed into our path and we excitedly passed the ball back trying our hardest to be accurate and not show ourselves up.

"I was in goal 'between the jumpers' Ian chased after a stray pass and shouted to me to see if I could save his shot. I gladly accepted his challenge and he blasted a rocket straight at me. I saved the shot, but the sound of the ball slapping against my bare hands was probably heard in Leeds city centre. The pain was shocking, but I didn't flinch and passed the ball back to him with the expression of a young kid trying not to cry, mixed with the smugness of a kid who had just saved a shot from a Leeds legend. He laughed because of the slapping sound and my strange expression, but congratulated me on my save and said next time he'd hit it harder as that was only a back pass.

"I couldn't wait to tell my dad, that I had saved a shot from Ian Baird."

### Glen Downing, Brighton & Hove Albion fan

"One of favourite moments of that incredible last season at the Goldstone Ground involved Ian Baird. The last ever floodlit game against Barnet when he scored the winning goal in front of the North Stand it seemed to come off of his knee about five yards out. His goal celebration was hilarious as he went running in front of the North Stand pointing to his knee.

"For me, that was the sign that lady luck was right behind us and we were going to stay up that season."

### Jon Howe, Leeds United fan

"Like an Action Man you got for Christmas, Ian Baird was the identikit Leeds United player for the 1980s. 14 year old kids weren't bothered about how you organised your teammates at a corner, or whether a player shook hands with the referee in a sporting manner after the game. We wanted blood and guts and a clenched fist to the Kop.

"In the 1980s, Ian Baird became one of my first heroes at a time when heroes were thin on the ground. He was fearless, committed and basically one of us; prowling the frontline menacingly like a Viking berserker.

"For the visit of high-flying Oxford United in April 1985, my brother Mike and I were allowed on to the unforgiving playground of the Elland Road Kop for the first time. We had graduated from the safety of the West Stand seats and had finally arrived.

"Table-topping Oxford were humbled 1-0 with Baird dispatching the decisive goal right in front of us. That morning I had been to school to retrieve a lost football from the school roof. In panic I had jumped from the roof and jolted my back on landing. I was in agony all day and totally unprepared for the involuntary joyous leap when Baird scored, and the subsequent melee of seemingly thousands of Leeds fans jumping all over me in celebration. It was pleasure and pain, it was the Kop, it was Ian Baird, it was the 1980s; it was perfect."

**Sven E. Malvaag, Leeds United fan (from Norway)**
"When Ian played for Leeds in the 80s, Norwegian television did not broadcast footage of games from England's second tier. I was stuck and in desperation to have information about my team, I went on to subscribe to the match day programmes. What a highlight to see my heroes 'in action'.

"I could see what John Sheridan, Ian Snodin, Ian Baird and all the rest of the team really looked like. It was a magic moment when those programmes arrived by post. I demanded a couple of hours free from schoolwork, just to be by myself and study these golden papers.

"That was my background. No television to watch my heroes, only the programmes and occasionally the radio with a bad reception.

"I contribute to an internet blog for Leeds United supporters in Scandinavia, discussing different matters. My user name on that forum is "Ian Baird", because I thought he always showed 100% passion and aggression."

**Michael Hewitt, Leeds United fan**
"I was attending a function held by the Rotherham Branch of the Leeds United Supporters Club where Ian Baird was a guest. He was being accosted about not playing well that afternoon. Ian stood up and gave as much as he was given. He had played ok, the criticism was bang out of order and I said so after Ian had left.

"In a bar after the Hapoel Tel Aviv v Leeds game in Florence, I had the pleasure of introducing some of our newer South Kirkby members to Ian. He seemed surprised we held him in our hearts still. But his 100% effort and goals will always be recognised.

"In 1987 in a game v Telford in the FA Cup, which should have been postponed, played at West Brom on a sheet of ice and snow. When others could not keep their feet, Ian Baird scored both goals in a 2-1 win.

"My favourite goal was in the 1986-87 season against Plymouth Argyle at home. A great move lead to Jackie Ashurst's cross being headed in by Bairdy to complete his hat-trick."

Ian signing a Leeds United handbook for Hilary Attard,
Leeds fan from Malta.

Ian with Paul Dunham on Fullerton Park.

An autograph hunter meets his hero.

Ian at the Kippax LUSC annual presentation night in 1986 with his mate Trevor and Leeds fans Andy 'Sid' Johnson, Stevie P and Martin 'Slugger' Johnson.

Ian at Elland Road in 2013 with Jon Howe, author of All White - Leeds United 100 Greatest and Marc Bracha, Ian's biographer.

Ian and Leeds fan Ben Scott in 2012.

**Gordon White, Hearts fan**

"The incident at Brechin showed Ian's passion and fearless attitude that he always displayed on the pitch. There weren't many Hearts fans there that night that would have had the bottle to tell the culprit, who was a big bloke, to put a lid on it and calm down.

"With Ian you always got 100%, and you knew he would be prepared to risk all for the team.

"I will always have fond memories of his time at Tynecastle."

**Patrick Bushell, Leeds United fan**

"I was 16 or 17 at the time and I went to Fullerton Park to watch Leeds train, Ian Baird walked past and I asked if I could have my photo taken with him, he duly obliged. I got the photo developed and blown up into poster, took it back to the ground and asked Ian to sign it. In addition to signing the poster, Ian asked me if he could have a copy, I got one done but didn't see him for a few weeks. Someone at the club told Ian that I was looking for him, he met me after one particular game and gave me £10 for the poster."

**David Smith, Brighton & Hove Albion fan.**

"When Ian Baird played for Brighton, I was seven years old and I wanted to share my one defining memory of him. He was always my favourite player during that, my first, season. There was a goal he scored where the ball was crossed to the back post (I'm not sure who against) in front of the South Stand and Ian chested it into the net from about four yards out. It was probably the most skilful piece of football I'd witnessed that season and it has stuck with me to this day. For about a year after, I was getting my dad to chip me the ball in our back garden as I constantly failed to chest it in the net a la Baird."

**Ray Fell, Chairman of the Leeds United Supporters Club**

"I well remember Ian's two spells with Leeds United in both of which he earned the warm support and backing of the supporters.

"I was honoured to present to Ian the Leeds United Supporters Club trophy for player of the year for the season ending 1988/89.

"Ian Baird was a player who never knew any other way of playing than to give 100% in every match and his effort is remembered constantly by the supporters who were present during that period. I still remember the fondness with which he was greeted on his second spell with the club.

"I am delighted that Ian is receiving this tribute and I know that the Leeds United Supporters Club members will support me wholeheartedly in thanking Ian for his past services to Leeds United and wishing him every success with the book and his own personal future."

**Ralph Ineson, Television star and a Leeds United fan**

"I remember him lifting the roof off Elland Road with a few tackles. He was the fans' representative on the pitch during some turgid times. The kind of fella you want by your side in most situations, on the pitch, in the trenches, or in the pub car park."

**Andy Wilson, Middlesbrough fan.**

"I always recall a game against Newcastle United, it was the last game of the season, we had to win to stay up and they had to win to go up. We battered them 4-1 and Bairdy got two. I remember him flicking his ears at their centre half as if to say he was a donkey."

**Paul Dews, Leeds United Head of Media and a Leeds United fan**

"When I was recently asked to name the five greatest players I had ever seen play for Leeds, I deliberated with throwing Ian's name in there. I'm sure he would understand when I say I didn't, but if I was asked to name my top five favourite players I had ever seen, his name would definitely be in there. Bairdy was my first ever Leeds hero and I still compare players' attitudes and work-rates to him nowadays. For me, he epitomised everything about being a Leeds United player and to have seen the majority of games he played for the club is something I'm proud of."

**Chris Webb, Plymouth Arygle fan.**

"I will always remember the FA Cup tie against Coventry who were down to 10 men.

Argyle went 1-0 up thanks to an Ian Baird free-kick and Home Park was electrifying."

**Gary Edwards, Leeds United fan.**

"A mate of mine has a great picture hanging proudly at the top of his staircase. It is a striking painting depicting a full house at Elland Road. The game is Leeds United v Newcastle United; the date is 2nd December 1989; the score is 1-0 to Leeds – and the scorer is Ian Baird. That brilliant diving header right in front of the Kop was Bairdy's last ever goal for United – but by then he had etched out a granite like memory that remains with every Leeds fan who was lucky enough to have seen him ply his trade in the opposing penalty areas up and down the country for six seasons.

"Baird was not only a prolific goalscorer however, and under the watchful eye of Leeds manager Billy Bremner, he also became a very effective and brave target man.

"I celebrated my 31st birthday in style thanks to Ian Baird.

"It was the 28th of March 1987 and Bairdy literally ripped Plymouth Argyle to shreds with a blistering performance – one of the best attacking displays I have ever seen – giving him a superb hat-trick. After the game, while Bairdy was polishing his match ball, some of the lads had arranged for me to have a photograph taken with Billy Bremner making it truly a day to cherish forever."

4534756R00127

Printed in Great Britain
by Amazon.co.uk, Ltd.,
Marston Gate.